the language of learning

FINDLEY

of learning

A GUIDE

TO EDUCATION

TERMS

J. LYNN MCBRIEN
AND RONALD S. BRANDT
with editorial consultation from Robert W. Cole

ASSOCIATION FOR SUPERVISION
AND CURRICULUM DEVELOPMENT

ALEXANDRIA, VIRGINIA

Association for Supervision and Curriculum Development
1250 N. Pitt Street • Alexandria, Virginia 22314-1453
Telephone: 1-800-933-2723 or 703-549-9110 • Fax: 703-299-8631

Gene R. Carter, *Executive Director*
Michelle Terry, *Assistant Executive Director, Program Development*
Ronald S. Brandt, *Assistant Executive Director*
Nancy Modrak, *Director, Publishing*
John O'Neil, *Acquisitions Editor*
Julie Houtz, *Managing Editor of Books*
Kathie Felix, *Associate Editor*
Gary Bloom, *Director, Design, Editorial, and Production Services*
Karen Monaco, *Senior Designer*
Tracey A. Smith, *Production Coordinator*
Dina Murray, *Production Assistant*
Valerie Sprague, *Desktop Publisher*

Copyright © 1997 by the Association for Supervision and Curriculum
Development. All rights reserved. No part of this publication may be
reproduced or transmitted in any form or by any means, electronic or
mechanical, including photocopy, recording, or any information storage
and retrieval system, without permission from ASCD. Readers who wish
to duplicate material copyrighted by ASCD may do so for a small fee by
contacting the Copyright Clearance Center, 222 Rosewood Dr., Danvers,
MA 01923, USA (phone: 508-750-8400; fax: 508-750-4470). ASCD has
authorized the CCC to collect such fees on its behalf. Requests to reprint
rather than photocopy should be directed to ASCD's permissions office at
(703) 549-9110.

ASCD publications present a variety of viewpoints. The views expressed
or implied in this book should not be interpreted as official positions of
the Association.

Printed in the United States of America.

s6/97
ASCD Stock No.: 197155
ASCD member price: $11.95   nonmember price: $13.95

Library of Congress Cataloging-in-Publication Data
McBrien, J. Lynn.
    The language of learning : a guide to education terms / J. Lynn
McBrien and Ronald S. Brandt ; with editorial consultation from
Robert W. Cole.
        p.   cm.
        Includes bibliographical references and index.
        ISBN 0-87120-274-3 (pbk.)
        1. Education—Dictionaries. 2. Education—Terminology.
    I. Brandt, Ronald S. II. Cole, Robert W., 1945-   . III. Title.
    LB15.M32   1997
    370 :3—dc21   97-19649
                                                        CIP

01 00 99 98 97   5 4 3 2 1

The Language of Learning:
A Guide to Education Terms

Foreword

Cooperative learning. OBE. Goals 2000. Magnet schools. What on earth are they? Educators and government officials use these terms and many others every day. They reflect important aspects of the education of U.S. schoolchildren—yet parents and other concerned adults frequently do not know what they mean.

Last September I called the superintendent's office in one of the best school districts in New Hampshire to ask where I might watch a satellite transmission of a *Goals 2000* meeting. The secretary had never heard of *Goals 2000*. A Public Agenda report (*First Things First*, 1994) quotes a father talking about OBE: "Outcome-based education? That's sort of on the idea where the students are all in the classroom, and they decide the way it's going to be and [assign] their own grades." And while doing final edits on this book, I stopped by a pharmacy for a couple items. The clerk at the register mentioned that she noticed lots of kids out of school that day. I told her it was a teacher's professional day. "Oh," she said, "I remember those from my teaching days. We used to hate them. We never had any idea what the presenters were talking about."

Why do we clutter communication with so much jargon? Certainly educational jargon has its place, just as special language is useful in medicine, law, technology, and other professions. Jargon is a type of shorthand; it allows us to economize on words with our peers. Jargon should help us communicate with precision, although the words may be unintelligible to those outside the given profession. It makes sense, for example, for teachers to talk among themselves about performance assessments and assume that they have the same basic idea about those assessments.

The problem, of course, is when educators have different understandings about what these terms mean. Additionally, some terms take on loaded connotations over time. For instance, OBE pioneer William Spady argues that people's current understanding of the term "outcome-based education" has almost nothing to do with what the term was coined to describe.

Additionally, parents and other citizens cannot form intelligent opinions about school reform if they don't understand what is being discussed. It's worse if parents think they understand, but are really misinterpreting and misusing terms. The purpose of this book is to enlighten parents, school board members, business leaders, and other concerned citizens about educational jargon in an objective way, using everyday language. Each entry offers a definition, and some entries include examples and resources for more information.

At the end of the book you'll find topics with a list of key words related to that subject. You can use the list as a cross-reference and as a resource. For example, parents of a learning disabled child can use that list to give them a basic idea of words that may be used by school specialists when discussing the child. The information in the definitions may help the parents understand the situation and prepare them for discussing the challenges and options. The school specialists benefit from discussing the situation with informed parents.

As you glance through the book, you'll notice that some words appear in small capital letters. This indicates that the term is explained in a separate entry. You may want to refer to that entry for additional or related information. The topic list in the back may also be helpful in guiding you to the term you seek and related terms.

J. Lynn McBrien

Acknowledgments

I have many people to thank for bringing this project to fruition. Thanks go to the ASCD staff for believing in my ability to pull together a glossary that makes education rhetoric understandable to a layperson. Also, I want to express appreciation to my co-workers at the Educational Publishing Group for their encouragement. My greatest thanks go to my dear friend and the editor of this book, Bob Cole, who has supported me through the whole process with his editing skills and infinite kindness, patience, and trust.

J. Lynn McBrien

D efining terms used in education is hazardous because people mean different things when they use these words. We
would like this publication to be as complete, accurate,
and helpful as possible. If you come across a term you think
should have been in this book, or if you think one of our definitions is unclear or (even worse) wrong, please contact the authors
at the address on page 114, or the Managing Editor, Books at
ASCD. We'll try to improve in the second edition -- if there is one.

ability grouping See HOMOGENEOUS GROUPING.

accountability The responsibility of an agency to its clientele; specifically, to accomplish its mission with wise use of resources. In education, accountability is often understood to be measurable proof that teachers, schools, districts, and states are teaching students efficiently and well, usually illustrated in the form of student success rates on various tests. Accountability may be measured in terms of goals, which often state that students are to master a common core of knowledge and skills and, by implication, that school personnel are responsible for making sure students do so. Schools are judged on their results, as well as on their use of funds, productivity, and implementation of programs.

Critics argue that the practices and measures of some accountability programs are too simple and that they ignore complications caused by the social barriers that keep many schools from receiving adequate funding, especially poor and inner-city schools.

Educators debate the proper tools of accountability. Some support a prescribed curriculum assessed with traditional standardized testing. Others, because they emphasize processes and holistic learning, maintain that standardized tests are not an appropriate way to measure a child's learning.

Resources: "Accountability and the Struggle Over What Counts," by P. Theobald and E. Mills. *Phi Delta Kappan,* February 1995, pp. 462–466.

Communicating Student Learning: 1996 ASCD Yearbook, edited by T.R. Guskey. Available from ASCD, 1250 N. Pitt St., Alexandria, VA 22314-1453, tel. 703/549-9110, or 800/933-2723. Internet: http://www.ascd.org

How to Conduct a Formative Evaluation, by B. Beyer. Available from ASCD, 1250 N. Pitt St., Alexandria, VA 22314-1453, tel. 703/549-9110, or 800/933-2723. Internet: http://www.ascd.org

"The *Other* Kind of Report Card: When Schools Are Graded," by R.M. Jaeger, B.E. Gorney, and R.L. Johnson. *Educational Leadership,* October 1994, pp. 42–45.

Results: The Key to Continuous School Improvement, by M. Schmoker. Available from ASCD, 1250 N. Pitt St., Alexandria, VA 22314-1453, tel. 703/549-9110, or 800/933-2723. Internet: http://www.ascd.org

Tracking Your School's Success: A Guide to Sensible Evaluation, by J.L. Herman and L. Winters. Newbury Park, Ca.: Corwin Press.

2

achievement tests Tests used to measure how much a student has learned in various key subjects. Most students take several standardized achievement tests, such as the California Achievement Tests and the Iowa Achievement Tests. These NORM-REFERENCED, multiple-choice tests are intended to measure students' achievement in the basic subjects found in most school districts' CURRICULA and textbooks. Results are used to compare the scores of individual students and schools with others—those in the area, across the state, and throughout the United States.

Resources: California Achievement Tests, CTB Macmillan/McGraw-Hill, 2500 Garden Road, Monterey, CA 93940-5380.

A Teacher's Guide to Performance-Based Learning and Assessment, by Educators in Connecticut's Pomperaug School District 15. Available from ASCD, 1250 N. Pitt St., Alexandria, VA 22314-1453, tel. 703/549-9110, or 800/933-2723. Internet: http://www.ascd.org

action research Commonly refers to teachers' systematic investigation of some aspect of their work in order to solve a problem or to improve their effectiveness. Action research involves identifying a problem and collecting and analyzing relevant data. For example, a teacher who gives students different assignments according to their assessed learning styles and maintains records comparing their performances before and after the change is doing action research. A project with several educators working together is collaborative action research.

active learning   Any situation in which students move around and do things, rather than sitting at their desks, reading, filling out worksheets, or listening to a teacher. Active learning is based on the premise that, if students are not active, they are neither fully engaged nor learning as much as they could. Some educators restrict the term active learning to activities outside of school, such as voluntary community service, but others would say that acting out a Shakespeare play in the classroom is active learning.

See also INTERACTIVE LEARNING, MANIPULATIVES, and PERFORMANCE TASKS.

Resources: *Inspiring Active Learning: A Handbook for Teachers,* by M. Harmin. (1994). Available from ASCD, 1250 N. Pitt St., Alexandria, VA 22314-1453, tel. 703/549-9110, or 800/933-2723. Internet: http://www. ascd. org

Promoting Active Learning: Strategies for the College Classroom, by C. Meyers and T.B. Jones. Available from Jossey-Bass Publishers, 350 Sansome St., San Francisco, Ca. 94104, tel. 415/433-1740, or 800/957-7739. Internet: http://www.josseybass.com

ADA See AVERAGE DAILY ATTENDANCE.

Advanced Placement (AP) Program   College-level courses offered by many high schools to students who are above average in academic standing.

If a student passes a standardized AP test, most colleges will award credit for the equivalent college course. (A student does not necessarily have to take an AP course in the subject.) Passing AP tests can save the student time and tuition on entry-level college courses.

In addition, some high schools make arrangements with local colleges for advanced students to take college courses for credit. Local college credits may transfer to other institutions.

advisory system   A way of organizing schools so that all students have an adult advisor who knows them well and sees them frequently. Although most schools have trained counselors, the counselors work with hundreds of students, and cannot see any one student very often. To make advisory groups as small as possible, schools ask staff members who are not classroom teachers, sometimes including the principal, the librarian, or others, to serve as advisors. Most schools schedule periods of time, sometimes daily, for advisory groups to meet for group and individual activities.

affective education   Schooling that helps students deal in a positive way with their emotions and values is sometimes called affective to distinguish it from COGNITIVE LEARNING, which is concerned with facts and ideas. Although the two can be discussed and even taught separately, we know that the mind stores memories in many ways, and that for individuals, everything we learn has emotional connections. For example, when we think of Shakespeare's play *Romeo and Juliet,* we call up not only the plot but also how we feel about it, including how we may have felt about studying it in high school.

4

alternative scheduling   Sometimes called block scheduling, alternative scheduling is a way of organizing the school day, usually in secondary schools, into blocks of time longer than the typical 50-minute class period. Students take as many courses as before (sometimes more), but the courses do not run the entire school year. One alternative schedule used in some secondary schools, known as 4x4, has four ninety-minute classes a day with course changes every 45 days (four times a school year). Students and teachers have to prepare for fewer classes and experience fewer interruptions in the school day. Longer blocks of time allow for learning activities, including complicated science experiments and other projects.

See also FLEXIBLE SCHEDULING.

Resource: *Alternative Scheduling.* Video series. Available from ASCD, 1250 N. Pitt St., Alexandria, VA 22314-1453, tel. 703/549-9110, or 800/933-2723. Internet: http://www.ascd.org

alternative schools   Schools that are different in one or more ways from traditional public schools. Alternative schools may reflect a particular teaching philosophy, such as MULTIDISCIPLINARY CURRICULUM, or a specific focus, such as science and technology. Alternative schools may operate under different governing principles than traditional schools and be run by groups other than local school boards.

The term alternative schools is often used to describe schools that are designed primarily for students who have been unsuccessful in regular schools, either because of disabilities or behavioral or emotional difficulties. Mary Anne Raywid, an authority on alternative schools, argues against establishing last chance or remedial schools in which the students are seen as a problem to be fixed. Raywid believes that a better approach is to alter the program and environment to create a positive match with each student.

See also CHARTER SCHOOLS, MAGNET SCHOOLS, and PRIVATIZED SCHOOLS.

Resources: "Alternative Schools: The State of the Art," by M.A. Raywid. *Educational Leadership,* September 1994, pp. 26–31.

Don't Tell Us It Can't Be Done!, edited by C. Chamberlin. Available from the Resource Center for Redesigning Education, P. O. Box 298, Brandon, VT 05733-0298, tel. 802/247-4294, or 800/639-4122. E-mail: holistic@sover.net.

alternative teacher certification　A way for individuals to become classroom teachers without completing an undergraduate or graduate program in teacher education. Alternative certification takes into account an individual's background and experience and usually requires some professional training in the first years of teaching.

Alternative paths to certification allow more adults to enter the teaching profession, especially those who have a liberal arts background and who desire a new and challenging career. Alternative certification is most common in inner-city and rural settings, where teachers are more in demand.

Resources: Recruiting New Teachers, 385 Concord Avenue, Belmont, MA 02178, tel. 617/489-6000.

Teach for America program, AmeriCorps, 1201 New York Ave. NW, Washington, DC 20525, tel. 800/942-2677; TDD no. 800/833-3722. Internet: http://www.cns.gov

American College Test (ACT)　A test that is similar to the SCHOLASTIC ASSESSMENT TEST (SAT) and also is used for admission to college. Created and operated by ACT Corp., the ACT assessment attempts to "measure those higher-order thinking skills that are taught across the curriculum and are necessary to succeed in post-secondary education settings." The exam contains four parts: English, reading, math, and science reasoning. More than 1.5 million college-bound students take the ACT each year.

　　Resources: ACT Corp., 2201 N. Dodge St., P.O. Box 168, Iowa City, IA 52243, tel. 319/337-1000.

　　The *Official Guide for the ACT Assessment.* Available from Harcourt, Brace, Jovanovich, 6277 Sea Harbor Drive, Orlando, FL 32887, tel. 407/345-2000, or 800/225-5425.

AmeriCorps　A centerpiece of the National and Community Service Trust Act signed into law by President Clinton on Sept. 21, 1993, the AmeriCorps programs provide money for additional education in exchange for full-time service. The programs are open to U.S. citizens who have received a high school diploma or GENERAL EDUCATIONAL DEVELOPMENT (GED) diploma. Two of the main programs are AmeriCorps*VISTA, a service program for individuals 18 and older, and AmeriCorps*National Civilian Community Corps (NCCC), which seeks U.S. citizens 18 to 24 years old for community service in a residential setting.

　　During their period of service, members receive housing, meals, a modest stipend, and limited health care. VISTA members serve in low-income areas and help community members improve their lives and communities by finding housing opportunities, developing literacy programs, establishing credit unions, and improving available health care. NCCC members work in teams of 10–14, focusing on one of four areas: the environment, education, public safety, or other human needs.

　　In exchange for a year of full-time service, AmeriCorps members receive a $4,725 education award to be applied to technical training, a college education, or existing college loans.

　　Resources: AmeriCorps, 1201 New York Ave. NW, Washington, DC 20525, tel. 800/942-2677; TDD no. 800/833-3722. Internet: http://www.cns.gov

　　Education and AmeriCorps: A Guide to Connecting Service and Learning. Available from Education Commission of the States, Suite 2700, 707 17th St., Denver, CO 80202-3427, tel. 303/299-3692.

aptitude tests   Tests that attempt to predict a person's ability to do something. The most familiar are Intelligence Quotient (IQ) tests, which are intended to measure a person's intellectual abilities. The theory underlying intelligence tests is that each person's intellectual ability is stable and cannot be changed much, if at all. Some aptitude tests measure a person's natural ability to learn particular subjects and skills or suitability for certain careers.

Advocates of Howard Gardner's MULTIPLE INTELLIGENCES theory maintain that IQ tests measure only linguistic and analytical reasoning and that the other intelligences are not tested by traditional methods.

The outcomes of aptitude tests reveal biases against minorities and women. Since 1979 the U.S. Court of Appeals has banned IQ testing of African-American children in California for placement into SPECIAL EDUCATION classes. The ban, challenged in 1992, was upheld by the Appeals Court for the Ninth Circuit (*FairTest EXAMINER,* Fall 1994, p. 6).

> **Resources:** *Fallout from the Testing Explosion,* by N. Medina and M. Neil. Available from FairTest, 342 Broadway, Cambridge, MA 02139-1802, tel. 617/864-4810.
>
> *Testing for Learning,* by R. Mitchell. Available from The Free Press, 866 Third Ave., New York, NY 10022, tel. 212/698-7000.

assessment   Measuring or judging the learning and performance of students or teachers. Different types of assessment instruments include ACHIEVEMENT TESTS and COMPETENCY TESTS, DEVELOPMENTAL SCREENING TESTS, APTITUDE TESTS, PERFORMANCE TASKS, and authentic assessments.

The effectiveness of a particular approach to assessment depends on its suitability for the intended purpose. For instance, multiple-choice, true or false, and fill-in-the-blank tests can be used to assess basic skills or to find out what students remember. To assess other skills, PERFORMANCE TASKS and PORTFOLIOS may be more appropriate.

Performance assessments require students to perform a task, such as writing a short business letter to inquire about a product, or serving a volleyball. Sometimes the task may be designed to assess the student's ability to apply knowledge learned in school. For example, a student might be asked to determine what types of plants could be grown in various soil samples by measuring the pH.

Authentic assessments are performance assessments that are not artificial or contrived. Educators who want assessments to be more authentic worry that most school tests are necessarily contrived. Writing a letter to an imaginary company only to demonstrate to the teacher that you know how is different from writing a letter to a real person or company in order to achieve a real purpose. One way to make an assessment more authentic is to have students choose the particular task they will use to demonstrate what they have learned. For example, a student might choose to demonstrate her understanding of a unit in chemistry by developing a model that illustrates the problems associated with oil spills. See also AUTHENTIC LEARNING.

Here are some terms related to assessment:

- Measurement error—The calculated amount by which a test score may vary from the student's true score (no test can be exact in measuring a student's ability).

- Reliability—An estimate of how closely the results of a test would match if the test was given repeatedly to the same student under the same conditions.

- Sampling—A way of estimating how a whole group would perform on a test by (1) testing representative members of the group, or (2) giving different portions of the test to various subgroups (matrix sampling).

- Validity—How well a test measures what it is intended to measure.

Resources: *Assessing Student Outcomes: Performance Assessment Using the Dimensions of Learning Model,* by R. Marzano, D. Pickering, and J. McTighe. Available from ASCD, 1250 N. Pitt St., Alexandria, VA 22314-1453, tel. 703/549-9110, or 800/933-2723. Internet: http://www.ascd.org

Assessing Student Performance: Exploring the Purpose and Limits of Testing, by G.P. Wiggins. Jossey-Bass Publishers, 350 Sansome St., San Francisco, CA 94104, tel. 415/433-1740, or 800/956-7739. Internet: http://www.josseybass.com

ERIC, Clearinghouse on Assessment and Evaluation, The Catholic University of America, 210 O'Boyle Hall, Washington, DC 20064, tel. 202/319-5120, or 800/464-3742. Fax 202/319-6692. Internet: http://www.cua.edu/www/eric_ae

Expanding Student Assessment, edited by Vito Perrone. Available from ASCD, 1250 N. Pitt St., Alexandria, VA 22314-1453, tel. 703/549-9110, or 800/933-2723. Internet: http://www.ascd.org

Educational Leadership, October 1994. Theme issue on "Reporting What Students Are Learning." Available from ASCD, 1250 N. Pitt St., Alexandria, VA 22314-1453, tel. 703/549-9110, or 800/933-2723. Internet: http://www.ascd.org

Responsive Assessment: A New Way of Thinking About Learning, by M. Henning-Stout. Available from Jossey-Bass Publishers, 350 Sansome St., San Francisco, Ca. 94104, tel. 415/433-1740, or 800/957-7739. Internet: http://www.josseybass.com

at-risk   Term used to refer to students who have a higher than average probability of dropping out or failing school. Broad categories usually include students who are not fluent in English; inner-city, low-income, and homeless children; and SPECIAL-NEEDS STUDENTS with emotional or behavioral difficulties. Substance abuse, juvenile crime, unemployment, poverty, and lack of adult support are thought to increase a youth's risk factor.

9

Many educators are uncomfortable using the term at-risk, arguing that it labels a child and may affect the way teachers, administrators, and peers view the student. Henry Levin, a Stanford University professor and founder of the Accelerated Schools Project (a model that encourages schools to speed up rather than slow the learning process for disadvantaged students), says

> Any time you start to sort out kids, you eventually build categories with given assumptions. If you start off saying this child is at risk, you're saying this child is defective. So we send the child to the repair shop. The problem is, you'll never make the child whole when you stigmatize the child in every possible way. You make the child see that he or she isn't as good as the others. And in the meantime, other kids are moving ahead. Once the child is in the repair shop, he or she will never be out of the repair shop. ("Full Speed Ahead," by Jonathan Weisman. *Teacher Magazine,* November/December 1994, pp. 44-49.)

Whatever the term, these children and teens need special attention and support that might include peer mediation (see CONFLICT RESOLUTION), professional counseling, tutors, MENTORS, and other caring adults who challenge them with high expectations. (See also EFFECTIVE SCHOOLS.)

Resources: The Bureau for At-Risk Youth, 135 Dupont St., Plainview, NY 11803, tel. 516/349-5520, or 800/99-YOUTH.

CRESPAR, Johns Hopkins University, CSOS, 3505 N. Charles St., Baltimore, MD 21218, fax 410/516-8890.

Henry M. Levin, Director, National Center for the Accelerated Schools Project, Stanford University, CERAS 109, Stanford, CA 94305-3084. Internet: http://www.leyland.stanford.edu/group/ASP

National Dropout Prevention Center, 205 Martin St., Clemson, SC 29634-0726, tel. 864/656-2599, or 800/443-6392. Internet: http://www. dropoutprevention.org

Teaching Advanced Skills to At-Risk Students, edited by B. Means, C. Chelemer, and M.S. Knapp. Published by Jossey-Bass Publishers, 350 Sansome St., San Francisco, CA 94104, tel. 415/433-1740, or 800/956-7739. Internet: http://www.josseybass.com

Trashcan Kids, by R. Benedict. Available from ASCD, 1250 N. Pitt St., Alexandria, VA 22314-1453, tel. 703/549-9110, or 800/933-2723. Internet: http://www.ascd.org

Using What We Know about At-Risk Youth: Lessons for the Field, edited by R. Morris. Lancaster, Pa.: Technomic Pub. Co.

10

Youth Violence: A Policymaker's Guide. Available from Education Commission of the States, Suite 2700, 707 17th St., Denver, CO 80202-3427, tel. 303/299-3692.

Attention Deficit (Hyperactivity) Disorder—(AD(H)D)

Children diagnosed with this disorder tend to have problems staying on task and focusing on conversations or activities. ADD children may be impulsive; easily distracted (e.g., by someone talking in another room, or by a passing car), full of unfocused energy, fidgety, and restless.

Many people with ADD are also hyperactive and may move rapidly from one task to another without completing any of them. Hyperactivity, a disorder of the central nervous system, makes it difficult for affected children to control their motor activities.

More than half of students with LEARNING DISABILITIES exhibit behaviors associated with attention problems, but do not necessarily have ADD.

Resources: *The ADD Hyperactivity Workbook: For Parents, Teachers, and Kids,* by H.C. Parker. Plantation, Fl.: Specialty Press.

Attention Deficit Hyperactivity Disorder: Questions and Answers for Parents, by G. S. Greenberg and W.F. Horn. Available from Research Press, P.O. Box 9177, Champaign, IL 61826, tel. 217/352-3273, or 800/519-2707.

CHADD (Children with Attention Deficit Disorder—an organization for children, adults, parents, teachers, and caretakers), tel. 954/587-3700. Internet: http://www.chadd.org

The Myth of the ADD Child: 50 Ways to Improve Your Child's Behavior and Attention Span Without Drugs, Labels, or Coercion, by T. Armstrong. E.P. Dutton, 375 Hudson St., New York, NY 10014, tel. 212/366-2000, or 800/526-0275.

authentic learning   Authentic learning commonly refers to learning about and testing real-life situations, that is, the "kinds of problems faced by adult citizens and consumers or professionals in the field," states Grant Wiggins. Many critics of traditional teaching complain that what is taught in school has little relationship to anything people do in the world outside of school; authentic teaching and learning attempt to overcome that problem.

Authentic learning must have real value and quality—that is, the tasks should be those done by professionals in the field. The problems require HIGHER-ORDER THINKING SKILLS. Students know what is expected before beginning their work, and there is no mystery about the problems, as there is with traditional test questions.

Authentic learning situations require teamwork, problem-solving skills, and the ability to organize and prioritize the tasks needed to complete the project. Consultation with others, including the instructor, is encouraged. The goal is to produce a high-quality solution to a real problem that is worthy of examination, not to see how much a student can remember. The result should be an excellent product or performance.

Resources: Assessing Student Performance, by G.P. Wiggins. Jossey-Bass Publishers, 350 Sansome St., San Francisco, CA 94104, tel. 415/433-1740, or 800/956-7739. Internet: http://www.josseybass.com

Authentic Assessment, edited by K. Burke. Available from ERIC, Clearinghouse on Assessment and Evaluation, The Catholic University of America, 210 O'Boyle Hall, Washington, DC 20064, tel. 202/319-5120, or 800/ 464-37642. Fax 202/319-6692. E-mail: eric_ae@cua.edu.

Redesigning Assessment. Videotapes and guides. Available from ASCD, 1250 N. Pitt St., Alexandria, VA 22314-1453, tel. 703/549-9110, or 800/933-2723. Internet: http://www.ascd.org

11

average daily attendance (ADA)   Measured at schools on pre-determined dates during the school year, the ADA is a factor in determining how much money schools will receive and is used by both the state and federal departments of education.

basal reader   Basal readers are textbooks and anthologies (collections of stories or other writings) used to teach beginning reading. Many basal readers used to have mostly stories written especially for teaching (only certain words were used, as in the Dick and Jane stories), but many now contain a wider variety of children's literature.

benchmark   A standard for judging a performance. Just as a carpenter might use marks on his workbench to measure how long a part should be, teachers and students can use benchmarks to determine the quality of a student's work. Some schools develop benchmarks to tell what students should know by a particular stage of their schooling; for example, "by the end of sixth grade, students should be able to locate major cities and other geographical features on each of the continents."

bilingual education   The use of two or more languages for instruction. In the United States, students in bilingual classes or programs have not acquired full use of the English language, so they are taught academic content in their native language while continuing to learn English.

Bilingual education is considered a good way of giving LEP (LIMITED ENGLISH PROFICIENCY) students access to the same CURRICULUM as other students. Bilingual education is also intended to allow LEP parents to remain involved in their children's studies.

Advocates believe that maintaining students' native language does not interfere with their learning of English; research over the last decade indicates that bilingual instruction helps students learn a second language. Bilingual education helps ensure equity in education, and has received various levels of political support since 1968 and the passage of Title VII, the Bilingual Education Act (part of the Elementary and Secondary Education Act), which provided funding for LEP students. Title VII does not require schools to use languages other than English.

Opponents of bilingual education are trying to make English the legal language of the United States and to reduce or eliminate bilingual programs. People who oppose bilingual education feel it is too expensive and that U.S. schools should not be responsible for teaching in more than one language.

14

Resources: "Bilingual Education," by Joan Montgomery Halford. *ASCD Infobrief,* March 1996.

A Commonsense Guide to Bilingual Education, by J. Lessow-Hurley. Available from ASCD, 1250 N. Pitt St., Alexandria, VA 22314-1453, tel. 703/549-9110, or 800/933-2723. Internet: http://www.ascd.org

Mirror of Language: The Debate on Bilingualism, by K. Hakuta. Available from Basic Books, 10 E. 53 St., New York, NY 10022, tel. 800/638-3030.

block grant   The result of combining funding for several separate programs (generally federal programs) into a much larger program with one set of requirements. A positive feature of a block is greater flexibility in allocating funds. When federal funds are released to states in the form of block grants, the individual states have greater power in allocating the funds. Advocates of block grants for dispensing federal dollars believe that states can better define and serve their own areas of need than can the federal government.

A negative feature of a block is that it is usually accompanied by reduced funding. In 1981, for example, more than 40 education programs with a total budget of more than $600 million were combined to create Chapter 2 of the Educational Consolidation and Improvement Act. In the process, the funding for Chapter 2 was reduced based on the theory that it costs less money to regulate spending through a central source than through many small channels. In the program's first year, Chapter 2 received $130 million less than the original programs.

block scheduling   A restructuring of the traditional school day—from 50-minute class periods to longer time slots. Students take fewer courses a day for less than a full school year, and the longer blocks of time allow them to complete in-depth study of each subject. See also ALTERNATIVE SCHEDULING.

brain-based learning   Approaches to schooling that rely on recent brain research to support and develop improved teaching strategies. Researchers theorize that the human brain is constantly searching for meaning and seeking patterns and connections. AUTHENTIC LEARNING situations increase the brain's ability to make connections and retain new information.

15

Teaching strategies that enhance brain-based learning include MANIPULATIVES, ACTIVE LEARNING, field trips, guest speakers, and real-life projects that allow students to use many LEARNING STYLES and MULTIPLE INTELLIGENCES. An INTERDISCIPLINARY CURRICULUM or integrated learning also reinforces brain-based learning, because the brain can better make connections when material is presented in an integrated way, rather than as isolated bits of information.

A relaxed, nonthreatening environment that removes students' fear of failure is considered best for brain-based learning. Research also documents brain plasticity, which is the notion that the brain grows and adapts in response to external stimuli.

Resources: *A Celebration of Neurons: An Educator's Guide to the Human Brain,* by R. Sylwester. Available from ASCD, 1250 N. Pitt St., Alexandria, VA 22314-1453, tel. 703/549-9110, or 800/933-2723. Internet: http://www.ascd.org

Translating Brain Research into Classroom Practice, presented by P. Wolfe. Audiotape. Available from ASCD, 1250 N. Pitt St., Alexandria, VA 22314-1453, tel. 703/549-9110, or 800/933-2723. Internet: http://www.ascd.org

business and school partnerships   Cooperative arrangements that vary in methods of participation, funding, and relationship between the school and business. Some businesses allow employees to volunteer in schools during working hours. Volunteers may help students in informal ways, such as teaching job skills that include teamwork and problem solving.

Other partnerships involve substantial funding for technology or teacher training. Businesses may designate specific uses for their financial support, such as AT-RISK programs, tutorials, summer programs, or MAGNET SCHOOLS, or they may provide funds after first reviewing proposals.

Businesses are frequently involved in SCHOOL-TO-WORK programs. Some adopt a school and provide funding, supplies, and volunteers. In some instances, a business may offer to help a school design policies and management and organizational procedures.

16   Some corporations are involved in large-scale education partnerships and reforms. IBM's Reinventing Education programs and AT&T's Learning Network are among the largest business-education initiatives in the United States. IBM has donated $25 million along with volunteers, research, and technology to states and districts with large-scale reforms that use technology and that result in higher standards for students. AT&T has announced a $150 million education initiative to begin wiring all U.S. public schools for INTERNET access.

Resources: The Employer's Promise Initiative, U.S. Department of Education, 600 Independence Ave., SW, Washington DC 20202, tel. 800/USA-LEARN, or 800/96-PROMISE.

On Target: Effective Parent Involvement Programs, U.S. Chamber of Commerce, Center for Workforce Preparation, 1615 H St. NW, Washington, DC 20062, tel. 202/463-5525.

Reinventing Education: Entrepreneurship in America's Public Schools, by L.V. Gerstner Jr. Available from E.P. Dutton, 375 Hudson St., New York, NY 10014, tel. 212/366-2000, or 800/526-0275.

California Achievement Tests (CATs)   See ACHIEVEMENT TESTS.

Carnegie unit(s)   A measurement used in traditional high schools to determine how much coursework a student has completed. Students need roughly 20 Carnegie units to graduate; one unit is equal to a traditional 50-minute class taken several times per week (usually five) throughout the school year. A one-semester course is usually worth one-half of a Carnegie unit.

The units were created and promoted by the Carnegie Foundation for the Advancement of Teaching. Today, many educators involved in school reform oppose the use of Carnegie units, arguing that the units are arbitrary and that some topics and projects should be studied in longer blocks of time (see ALTERNATIVE SCHEDULING).

Chapter 1   See TITLE I.

character education   Teaching children about basic human values including honesty, kindness, generosity, courage, freedom, equality, and respect. The goal is to raise children to become morally responsible, self-disciplined citizens. Problem solving, decision making, and conflict resolution are important parts of developing moral character. Through role playing and discussions, students can see that their decisions affect other people and things. SERVICE LEARNING is frequently a part of a comprehensive character education program intended to develop the values of generosity, kindness, and respect.

Some people feel that school is not the place for values and character education and argue that values should be taught in the home and places of worship. Advocates reply that modern lifestyles are eroding the amount of time that families devote to teaching values, and that character education counters the increasing violence among young people. Although people's beliefs differ greatly, a majority of people living in the United States (69 percent, according to a 1993 Gallup Poll) believe it is possible for the people in a community to agree on a basic set of values to be taught in the public schools.

A group that actively promotes character education is the Character Education Partnership, a coalition of educational and civic organizations with viewpoints that range from liberal to conservative.

Resources: Character Education Partnership, John Martin, Executive Director, 809 Franklin St., Alexandria, VA 22314, tel. 703/739-9515.

Developing a Character Education Program: One School District's Experience, by H.A. Huffman. Available from ASCD, 1250 N. Pitt St., Alexandria, VA 22314-1453, tel. 703/549-9110, or 800/933-2723. Internet: http://www.ascd.org

Educating for Character: How Our Schools Can Teach Respect and Responsibility, by T. Lickona. Bantam Books, 666 Fifth Ave., New York, NY 10103, tel. 212/765-6500, or 800/223-6834.

Moral Classrooms, Moral Children, by R. DeVries and B. Zan. Available from Teachers College Press, Columbia University, 1234 Amsterdam Ave., New York, NY 10003, tel. 212/678-3929.

National Issues Forum: Contested Values, prepared by the Public Agenda Foundation and the Kettering Foundation. Published by McGraw-Hill, 1221 Avenue of the Americas, New York, NY 10020, tel. 212/512-2000, or 800/338-3987.

Why Johnny Can't Tell Right from Wrong: Moral Illiteracy and the Case for Character Education, by W. Kilpatrick. Simon & Schuster Education Group, 200 Old Tappan Rd., Old Tappan, NJ 07675, tel. 201/236-7000, or 800/922-0579.

charter school   A self-governing educational facility that operates under contract between the school's organizers and the sponsors (e.g., local school boards and state boards of education). The organizers are often teachers, parents, or private organizations. The charter may detail the school's instructional design, methods of ASSESSMENT, management, and finances.

Charter schools usually receive government funding, may not charge tuition, must be nonsectarian and nondiscriminatory, and must be chosen by teachers, students, and parents. To renew their charters, these schools must prove that they meet the expectations of parents and their governing boards, continue to attract families, and retain and attract teachers. In exchange for ACCOUNTABILITY, charter schools are free from most state and local regulations, often including traditional teacher certification and CARNEGIE UNITS.

Resource: Charter Schools: What Are They Up To? Available from Education Commission of the States, Suite 2700, 707 17th St., Denver, CO 80202-3427, tel. 303/299-3692.

coaching   A term commonly used in athletics; educators also use it to refer to any situation in which someone helps someone else learn a skill. Mortimer Adler, who devised the PAIDEIA program, maintained that coaching is one of three basic modes of teaching (the other two are presenting and leading discussions). Coaching is also considered an important part of training programs in which teachers learn new teaching methods. A process in which teachers visit each other's classes to observe instruction and offer feedback is known as peer coaching.

Coalition of Essential Schools   The coalition is a high school–university partnership established at Brown University and founded by Theodore Sizer, professor of education at Brown and former dean of the Harvard Graduate School of Education. The coalition grew out of a study of U.S. secondary education sponsored by the National Association of Secondary School Principals and the National Association of Independent Schools.

The coalition does not recognize any one school as a model school, believing that schools must be unique to best serve their particular communities, faculties, and students. Instead, coalition schools accept a set of nine governing principles that include helping young people learn to use their minds well; mastering a limited number of essential skills and areas of knowledge, rather than striving for broad content coverage; holding all students accountable for the same goals (using various teaching styles to accommodate the different ways in which students learn); maintaining a teacher-to-student ratio that permits teachers to know students as individuals; and arranging for competitive teacher salaries, as well as substantial planning and training time.

The Coalition of Essential Schools supports the idea that students must prove their mastery of certain skills and knowledge, decided on by the faculty and administrators along with the community, in order to graduate. Mastery is not tied to earning a certain number of CARNEGIE UNITS or to a specified graduation age.

Resources: Coalition of Essential Schools, Box 1969, Brown University, Providence, RI 02912, tel. 401/863-3384.

Horace's School: Redesigning the American High School, by T.R. Sizer. Available from National Professional Resources, 25 South Regent St., Port Chester, NY 10573, tel. 914/937-8879, or 800/453-7461. Internet: http://www.nprinc.com

The World We Created at Hamilton High, by G. Grant. (1988). Available from Harvard University Press, 79 Garden St., Cambridge, MA 02138, tel. 617/495-2600.

cognitive development   The process, which begins at birth, of learning through sensory perception, memory, and observation. Cognitive development is often mentioned in discussions about ready-to-learn strategies, which refer to preparing preschool children for school and keeping school-age children prepared for school.

Children are born into cultures and backgrounds that affect what they learn as well as how they learn. Children from enriched environments (in which parents and caregivers read to and with them, teach them letters and numbers, and take them to plays and museums) come to school prepared to learn; children from impoverished or abusive backgrounds often lack most or all of these preschool advantages. Programs such as HEAD START and Parents as Teachers have the goal of enriching children from lower socioeconomic backgrounds so that they too can thrive in school.

Public schools must attempt to educate all children; therefore, schools have to develop and test teaching strategies to meet
the needs of diverse families. Basic premises include placing
learning into a meaningful context, providing situations in which
students can be active participants, and combining general information with specific learning situations.

Resources: A Parent's Guide to Early Childhood Education, by D.T.
Dodge and J. Phinney. Available from Redleaf Press, 450 N. Syndicate,
Suite 5, St. Paul, MN 55104, tel. 800/423-8309. Also available in
Spanish, *Guia para Madres y Padres de Familia sobre Educacion Pre-
Escolar a Temprana Edad.*

Caring: Supporting Children's Growth and *Ready or Not: What Parents
Should Know About School Readiness.* Available from the National
Association for the Education of Young Children (NAEYC), 1509 16th St.
NW, Washington, DC 20036, tel. 202/232-8777, or 800/424-2460.

cognitive learning   The mental processes involved in learning,
such as remembering and understanding facts and ideas.
Educators have always been interested in how people learn, but
are now becoming better informed about cognition from the work
of cognitive psychologists, who in recent years have compiled a
great deal of new information about thinking and learning.

21

cohort   A particular group of people with something in common.
For instance, a cohort might be a group of students who had
been taught an interdisciplinary curriculum by a team of junior
high school teachers. Researchers might want to track their
progress into high school to identify differences in success of students in the cohort compared with students who had attended
conventional classes in the same school.

collaboration   A relationship between individuals or organizations that enables the participants to accomplish goals more successfully than they could have separately. Educators are finding
that they must collaborate with others to deal with increasingly
complex issues. For example, schools and school systems often
form partnerships with local businesses or social service agencies
(see BUSINESS AND SCHOOL PARTNERSHIPS). Some schools are also
teaching students how to work with others on group projects as

well as how to work independently. Some educators use the term collaborative learning for what others call COOPERATIVE LEARNING.

common ground   Fundamental values or goals that people agree upon although they may disagree strongly on other matters. The term is used by the Freedom Forum First Amendment Center, a nonprofit agency devoted to defense of freedom of conscience, to describe a process for improving communication between public educators and their critics.

Resource: Freedom Forum First Amendment Center, 1207 18th Avenue South, Nashville, TN 37212, tel. 615/321-9588.

community center schools   Organizations that provide services, often including medical and dental services, nutrition classes, parent programs, and social services, as part of the school program for both students and families. Collaborations between schools and agencies create their own means of delivery and make services readily accessible to members of the community. Community center schools provide essential services that many families could not otherwise obtain due to lack of transportation, information, money, or time.

Goals of school-linked programs include bringing a sense of community to social and health services, teachers, and families. Community center schools offer a place for parents to gather informally, learn English, offer opinions, and volunteer. Options offered by these schools help urban parents feel more comfortable in meeting with teachers, becoming a part of the learning community, and taking part in their children's studies (which also improves their children's school success).

Resources: Full Service Schools: A Revolution in Health and Social Services for Children, Youth, and Families, by J. Dryfoos. Available from Jossey-Bass Publishers, 350 Sansome St., San Francisco, Ca. 94104, tel. 415/433-1740, or 800/957-7739. Internet: http://www.josseybass.com

School-Based Collaboration with Families: Constructing the Family-School-Agency Partnerships That Work, by J.B. O'Callaghan. Available from National Professional Resources, 25 South Regent St., Port Chester, NY 10573, tel. 914/937-8879, or 800/453-7461. Internet: http://www. nprinc.com

22

competency tests Tests created by a school district or state that students must pass before graduating. Competency tests are intended to ensure that graduates have reached minimum proficiency in certain areas that they will need as adults. Not all states require competency tests.

complex reasoning See HIGHER-ORDER THINKING SKILLS.

computer-assisted instruction (CAI) In its broadest sense, CAI refers to educational programs delivered through the use of computers and educational software. CAI may be offered as a supplement to regular instruction. See also INTEGRATED LEARNING SYSTEMS.

CAI has a specific meaning as it applies to SPECIAL-NEEDS STUDENTS. Many software programs and features have been designed to help students with dyslexia and poor fine-motor skills. Blind students can work on Braille keyboards and command the computer to call up their work as synthesized speech or as a Braille display. Students with physical challenges can operate computers by activating a switch with their head, foot, mouth, or the blink of an eye.

23

Resources: The National Center to Improve Practice, funded by the Office of Special Education Programs at the U.S. Department of Education, provides information about innovative uses of technology for students with disabilities, tel. 617/969-7100, ext. 2387.

RESNA is a contact organization for all state technology-assisted programs and grants, tel. 703/524-6686, ext. 313.

conflict resolution Most often refers to programs that teach students how to negotiate problems in a nonviolent way. Peer mediation is an effective technique through which children or teens teach other students nonviolent ways to work through a problem.

Core concepts of conflict resolution include recognizing that conflict exists and is a pathway to personal growth; learning skills to solve problems effectively and nonviolently; and understanding that there are alternative solutions to a problem.

One result of conflict resolution training is a boost in self-empowerment. Students become confident and make decisions and change behaviors without adult intervention. Many schools are introducing this type of training to prevent and reduce violence in the school.

Resources: *Adult Conflict Resolution.* Video series. Available from ASCD, 1250 N. Pitt St., Alexandria, VA 22314-1453, tel. 703/549-9110, or 800/933-2723. Internet: http://www.ascd.org

Broader Urban Involvement and Leadership Development, 1223 N. Milwaukee Ave., 2nd Floor, Chicago, IL 60622, tel. 773/227-2880.

Children's Creative Response to Conflict, 521 N. Broadway, Nyack, NY 10960, tel. 914/353-1796.

The Eight Essential Steps to Conflict Resolution: Preserving Relationships at Work, at Home, and in the Community, by D. Weeks. Los Angeles: J.P. Tarcher. Distributed by St. Martin's Press.

Reducing School Violence Through Conflict Resolution, by D.W. Johnson and R.T. Johnson. Available from ASCD, 1250 N. Pitt St., Alexandria, VA 22314-1453, tel. 703/549-9110, or 800/933-2723. Internet: http://www.ascd.org

Talk It Out: Conflict Resolution in the Elementary Classroom, by B. Porro. Available from ASCD, 1250 N. Pitt St., Alexandria, VA 22314-1453, tel. 703/549-9110, or 800/933-2723. Internet: http://www.ascd.org

24

constructivism An approach to teaching based on research about how people learn. Many researchers say that each individual "constructs" knowledge rather than receiving it from others.

Although people disagree about how to achieve constructive learning, constructive teaching is based on the belief that students learn best when they gain knowledge through exploration and ACTIVE LEARNING. Hands-on materials are used instead of textbooks, and students are encouraged to think and explain their reasoning instead of memorizing and reciting facts. Education is centered on themes and concepts and the connections between them, rather than isolated information. See also BRAIN-BASED LEARNING.

Resources: *Constructivism.* Video series. Available from ASCD, 1250 N. Pitt St., Alexandria, VA 22314-1453, tel. 703/549-9110, or 800/933-2723. Internet: http://www.ascd.org

In Search of Understanding: The Case for Constructivist Classrooms, by J.G. Brooks and M.G. Brooks. Available from ASCD, 1250 N. Pitt St., Alexandria, VA 22314-1453, tel. 703/549-9110, or 800/933-2723. Internet: http://www.ascd.org

Visual Tools for Constructing Knowledge, by D. Hyerle. Available from ASCD, 1250 N. Pitt St., Alexandria, VA 22314-1453, tel. 703/549-9110, or 800/933-2723. Internet: http://www.ascd.org

continuous progress   A system of education in which individuals or small groups of students go through a sequence of lessons at their own pace, rather than at the pace of the entire classroom group. Continuous progress has also been called INDIVIDUALIZED EDUCATION or INDIVIDUALIZED INSTRUCTION and is one version of MASTERY LEARNING.

In continuous-progress programs, able and motivated students are not held back, and students take on new lessons only if they show they have the prerequisite skills. A criticism, however, is that unmotivated students often progress more slowly than they would in regular classes.

cooperative learning   A teaching strategy designed to imitate real-life learning and problem solving by combining teamwork with individual and group accountability. Working in small groups, with individuals of varying talents, abilities, and backgrounds, students are given a variety of tasks. The teacher or the group assigns each team member a personal responsibility that is essential to successful completion of the task.

25

Cooperative learning allows students to acquire both knowledge and social skills. The students learn from each other and get to know and respect group members that they may not have made an effort to meet in other circumstances. Studies show that, used properly, cooperative learning boosts student achievement. Schools using this strategy report that attendance improves because the students feel valuable and necessary to their group.

Resources: *Cooperative Learning,* by S. Kagan. Available from the Resource Center for Redesigning Education, P.O. Box 298, Brandon, VT 05733-0298, tel. 802/247-4294, or 800/639-4122. E-mail: holistic@sover.net.

Cooperative Learning in the Classroom, by D. Johnson, R. Johnson, and E.J. Holubec. Available from ASCD, 1250 N. Pitt St., Alexandria, VA 22314-1453, tel. 703/549-9110, or 800/933-2723. Internet: http://www.ascd.org

The New Circles of Learning: Cooperation in the Classroom and School, by D. Johnson, R. Johnson, and E. Johnson Holubec. Available from ASCD, 1250 N. Pitt St., Alexandria, VA 22314-1453, tel. 703/549-9110, or 800/933-2723. Internet: http://www.ascd.org

Readings from Educational Leadership: Cooperative Learning and the Collaborative School, edited by R.S. Brandt. Available from ASCD, 1250 N. Pitt St., Alexandria, VA 22314-1453, tel. 703/549-9110, or 800/933-2723. Internet: http://www.ascd.org

core curriculum   The body of knowledge that all students are expected to learn. High schools often require a core curriculum that includes four years of English, three years of science and math, two or three years of history, one or two years of a foreign language, and one year of health studies. Courses that are not required are called electives.

Core curriculum has also been used to refer to a block-of-time program in which students and their teacher choose the topics they study.

core knowledge   Refers specifically to a reform movement founded by E.D. Hirsch, author of *Cultural Literacy: What Every American Needs to Know.* The movement is based on the idea that there is a body of knowledge that students and citizens need to know to be culturally literate (see CULTURAL LITERACY), therefore school districts should offer a sequential, uniform CURRICULUM. Such a curriculum is offered in the *Core Knowledge Resource Series,* a collection of books that specify what students at each grade level should know.

Opponents argue that schools should emphasize the process of learning and the skills of gathering information, and place less emphasis on coverage of particular content.

Another argument concerns determining the content that all students should learn: Who should decide the core curriculum? Using what guidelines? The inclusion of certain topics, literary pieces, or historic events and the exclusion of others raises concerns about creating a fair and equitable course of study.

Resource: Core Knowledge Foundation, 2012-B Morton Drive, Charlottesville, VA 22903, tel. 804/977-7550.

criterion-referenced tests Tests designed to measure how thoroughly a student has learned a particular body of knowledge without regard to how well other students have learned it. Some states and school districts use criterion-referenced tests directly related to their curriculum, while most nationally standardized achievement tests are NORM-REFERENCED, meaning that a student's performance is compared to how well students in the norming group did when the test was normed.

critical thinking Logical thinking based on sound evidence; the opposite of biased, sloppy thinking. Some people take the word "critical" to mean negative and fault-finding, but Matthew Lipman, the philosopher who developed the Philosophy for Children program, describes critical thinking as "skillful and responsible." A critical thinker can accurately and fairly explain a point of view that he or she may not agree with. See HIGHER-ORDER THINKING SKILLS.

27

Resource: "Critical Thinking: What Can It Be?" by M. Lipman. *Educational Leadership*, September 1988, pp. 38–43.

cultural literacy The idea, set forth by E.D. Hirsch in *Cultural Literacy: What Every American Needs to Know*, that there is a certain body of knowledge that people must know to be well-educated, well-rounded U.S. citizens. See also CORE KNOWLEDGE.

Resource: Cultural Literacy: What Every American Needs to Know by E.D. Hirsch. Vintage Books, 201 E. 50th St., New York, NY 10022, tel. 212/751-2600, or 800/733-3000.

curricula plural of curriculum. (English plural is sometimes written as "curriculums.")

curriculum Usually refers to a written plan that outlines what students will be taught. Curriculum may refer to all the courses offered at a given school, or all the courses offered at a school in a particular area of study. For example, the English curriculum might include English literature, U.S. literature, world literature, essay styles, creative writing, business writing, Shakespeare, modern poetry, and the novel. The curriculum of an elementary school usually includes language arts, mathematics, science, and social studies.

Resources: *Content of the Curriculum,* edited by A.A. Glatthorn (2nd edition). ASCD, 1250 N. Pitt St., Alexandria, VA 22314-1453, tel. 703/549-9110, or 800/933-2723. Internet: http://www.ascd.org

The Curriculum Handbook and the *ASCD Curriculum/Technology* newsletter. Available as a subscription from ASCD, 1250 N. Pitt St., Alexandria, VA 22314-1453, tel. 703/549-9110, or 800/933-2723. Internet: http://www.ascd.org

Developing a Quality Curriculum, by A.A. Glatthorn. Available from ASCD, 1250 N. Pitt St., Alexandria, VA 22314-1453, tel. 703/549-9110, or 800/933-2723. Internet: http://www.ascd.org

Toward a Coherent Curriculum, The 1995 ASCD Yearbook, edited by J.A. Beane. Available from ASCD, 1250 N. Pitt St., Alexandria, VA 22314-1453, tel. 703/549-9110, or 800/933-2723. Internet: http://www.ascd.org

data-based decision making   Analyzing existing sources of **29** information (class and school attendance, grades, tests) and new data (portfolios, surveys, interviews) to make decisions about the school. The process involves organizing and interpreting the data and creating action steps. This approach can help educators explain the need for change to school board members and the community. See ACTION RESEARCH.

   Resources: Action Research: Inquiry, Reflection, and Decision Making. Video, book, and program guide. Available from ASCD, 1250 N. Pitt St., Alexandria, VA 22314-1453, tel. 703/549-9110, or 800/933-2723. Internet: http://www.ascd.org

   How to Conduct Collaborative Action Research by R. Sagor. Available from ASCD, 1250 N. Pitt St., Alexandria, VA 22314-1453, tel. 703/549-9110, or 800/933-2723. Internet: http://www.ascd.org

   How to Use Action Research in the Self-Renewing School, by E. Calhoun. Available from ASCD, 1250 N. Pitt St., Alexandria, VA, tel. 703/549/9110, or 800/933-2723. Internet: http://www.ascd.org

detracking   Reducing or eliminating grouping by ability, resulting in classes with students from all ability levels. The result of detracking is also called HETEROGENEOUS GROUPING rather than HOMOGENEOUS (or ability) GROUPING. Strictly speaking, tracking refers to students being lumped into groups for all their classes

based on their general ability to learn. Grouping for specific purposes, such as current knowledge of mathematics, is theoretically not tracking, but opponents, including Jeannie Oakes and
Anne Wheelock, charge that the practice usually has the same
results. Advocates of detracking, also called untracking, point to
research indicating that when students are grouped by ability,
those in lower tracks are usually taught poorly and don't get
exposed to "high status" knowledge. Advocates of grouping say it
is easier for teachers and better for students—both those who are
academically able and should not be held back, and those who
are slower and should have attention to their special needs.
Detracking advocates see it as part of a broader restructuring of
schools in which student differences are provided for within each
class. (See also TRACKING).

30

    *Resources: Crossing the Tracks: How 'Untracking' Can Save
America's Schools,* by A. Wheelock. New York: The New Press. Distributed
by W.W. Norton.
    How to Untrack your School, by P. George. Available from ASCD, 1250
N. Pitt St., Alexandria, VA 22314-1453, tel. 703/549-9110, or 800/933-
2723. Internet: http://www.ascd.org

developmental screening tests   Used to identify students who
may have disabilities, sensory impairments (e.g., near-sighted-
ness or reduced hearing), or behavioral and developmental disabilities.

developmentally appropriate education   Curriculum and
instruction that is in accord with the physical and mental development of the student. Developmentally appropriate education is
especially important for young children since their physical and
mental abilities change quickly and with great variation from
child to child. For example, some four-year old children are able
to sit quietly through a group story time, while others become fidgety. This does not necessarily mean that the more active children have ADHD; their neurological functions may simply not
have matured as quickly as others in their age group.
    Resources: Ages and Stages, by K. Miller. Available from Redleaf
Press, Suite 5, 450 N. Syndicate, St. Paul, MN 55104, tel. 800/423-8309.
    *Creating the Developmentally Appropriate School Using Constructivist
Principles of Leadership and Staff Development.* Audiotape series.

Available from ASCD, 1250 N. Pitt St., Alexandria, VA 22314-1453, tel. 703/549-9110, or 800/933-2723. Internet: http://www.ascd.org

Touchpoints: The Essential Reference, by T.B. Brazelton, M.D. Available from Addison-Wesley Publishing Co., Route 128, Reading, MA 01867, tel. 800/447-2226.

differentiated staffing   The practice of having different instructional roles rather than treating all classroom teachers alike. Various people play a part in the teaching process, but their responsibilities and pay may be greater or lesser than regular teachers. Typical roles include teacher aides, paraprofessionals (or assistant teachers), team leaders, and LEAD TEACHERS.

differentiated supervision   A system of supervising teachers that depends on factors including their experience, proven teaching ability, interests, and preferences. Some members of the teaching staff may be involved in clinical supervision (intensive analysis of their teaching based on observations of their classroom teaching), while others may propose and conduct their own PROFESSIONAL DEVELOPMENT plans.

31

Resources: *Clinical Supervision: Coaching for Higher Performance*, edited by R. Anderson and K. Snyder. Lancaster, Pa.: Technomic Pub. Co.

Differentiated Supervision, 2nd ed., by A. Glatthorn. Available from ASCD, 1250 N. Pitt St., Alexandria, VA 22314-1453, tel. 703/549-9110, or 800/933-2723. Internet: http://www.ascd.org

Peer Coaching for Educators, by B. Gottesman and J. Jennings. Lancaster, Pa.: Technomic Pub. Co.

Dimensions of Learning   An instructional model based on the theory that five types of learning are essential to the learning process. The five types are:

1. Positive attitudes and perceptions about learning.
2. Thinking involved in acquiring and integrating knowledge.
3. Thinking required in extending and refining knowledge.
4. Thinking involved in using knowledge meaningfully.
5. Productive HABITS OF MIND.

Resources: *A Different Kind of Classroom: Teaching with Dimensions of Learning*, by R. Marzano. Available from ASCD, 1250 N. Pitt St., Alexandria, VA 22314-1453, tel. 703/549-9110, or 800/933-2723. Internet: http://www.ascd.org

Dimensions of Learning Teacher's Manual, by R. Marzano and others. ASCD, 1250 N. Pitt St., Alexandria, VA 22314-1453, tel. 703/549-9110, or 800/933-2723. Internet: http://www.ascd.org

discovery learning   See ACTIVE LEARNING.

distance learning   Taking classes in locations other than the classroom or other place where the teacher presents the lesson. Various forms of technology, especially television and computers, are used in providing educational materials and experiences to students. Small high schools may arrange for their students to take courses, such as those for advanced foreign language instruction, by television. Many colleges and universities broadcast credit courses for students who live in isolated locations or who for other reasons cannot attend classes on campus.

   Resource: For information on the Public Broadcasting System college courses, tel. 703/739-5073, or 202/667-0901.

32

diversity   In education, discussions about diversity involve recognizing a variety of student needs including those of ethnicity, language, socioeconomic class, disabilities, and gender. School reforms attempt to address these issues to help all students to succeed, regardless of their unique characteristics. In addition, schools are beginning to recognize and promote the positive experiences that occur in diverse school populations, such as the sharing of cultural beliefs, experiences, and languages. See also MULTICULTURAL EDUCATION.

   Resources: Affirming Diversity: The Sociopolitical Context of Multicultural Education, by S. Nieto. New York: Longman.

   How to Respond to Your Culturally Diverse Student Population, by S.L. Wyman. Available from ASCD, 1250 N. Pitt St., Alexandria, VA 22314-1453, tel. 703/549-9110, or 800/933-2723. Internet: http://www.ascd.org

dyslexia   A condition that hampers reading ability. Characteristics of dyslexia may include

   • Transposing letters and numbers when reading and writing.

   • Confusing hand dominance.

   • Difficulty in keeping track of the order of time, months, or seasons.

- Hyperactivity.
- Difficulty with physical coordination and balance.

The cause of dyslexia is unknown. The results are difficulty in communicating and frustration for the child, classmates, and many teachers. Students with dyslexia need special resources and learning techniques to progress with their peers. Boys are four times more likely than girls to have this learning disability.

Resources: Council for Exceptional Children, Division on Mental Retardation and Developmental Disabilities, 1920 Association Drive, Reston, VA 20191-1589, tel. 703/620-3660.

Dyslexia Memorial Institute, 936 S. Michigan Ave., Chicago, IL 60612.

National Education Association, 1201 16th St., N.W., Washington, DC 20036, tel. 202/833-4000.

early childhood education   The education of young children. Many educators think of early childhood education as including children ages 3 through 7. Recent research information about the brain development of infants is causing many specialists to think of this period of rapid learning as beginning at birth.

Resources: Beginnings and Beyond: Foundations in Early Childhood Education, by A. Gordon and K. Browne. Albany, N.Y.: Delmar Publishers.

Early Childhood Education, Video series. Available from ASCD, 1250 N. Pitt St., Alexandria, VA 22314-1453, tel. 703/549-9110, or 800/933-2723. Internet: http://www.ascd.org

Starting Points: Meeting the Needs of Our Youngest Children. Available from the Carnegie Corporation of New York, 437 Madison Ave., New York, NY 10022, tel. 212/371-3200. Internet: http://www.carnegie.org

Understanding Child Development: For Adults Who Work with Young Children, by R. Charlesworth. Albany, N.Y.: Delmar Publishers.

Edison schools   Schools run by the Edison Project, a private organization under contract with local boards of education. All Edison schools (named to commemorate inventor Thomas Edison) are expected to follow the model developed by a design team headed by Benno Schmidt, former president of Yale University. Features of the model include extensive use of technology, individualized learning plans, teaching of values, and parent and community participation. Originally founded by Christopher Whittle, the Edison Project is an example of the privatization of public schools. See PRIVATIZED SCHOOLS.

   Resource: "The Edison Project's Plan to Redefine Public Education," by B.C. Schmidt Jr. *Educational Leadership,* September 1994, pp. 61–65.

Educate America Act   See GOALS 2000: EDUCATE AMERICA ACT.

Education Commission of the States   A nonprofit organization whose purpose is to "help governors, state legislators, state education officials, and others develop policies to improve the quality of education at all levels." The commission was formed in 1965 to help states approach education policy decisions in an organized fashion. Montana is the only state not a member of the ECS.

   The organization's current priorities include the setting of clear, high standards; increasing reform efforts in schools; supporting collaborations among schools and other education and social services; and furthering bipartisan support and public involvement in reform.

   Resource: Education Commission of the States, Suite 2700, 707 17th St., Denver, CO 80202-3427, tel. 303/299-3600.

effective schools   Schools in which all students, especially those from families in poverty, learn at a higher-than-expected level. The idea of effective schools was pioneered in the early 1980s by the late Ronald Edmonds, who compared schools in which children in poverty earned high test scores with other schools that had similar student populations. He found that effective schools had strong principals who closely monitored student achievement and created an orderly environment characterized by high expectations.

   Resources: Effective Schools for Children at Risk, video series. Available from ASCD, 1250 N. Pitt St., Alexandria, VA 22314-1453, tel. 703/549-9110, or 800/933-2723. Internet: http://www.ascd.org

   "Effective Schools for the Urban Poor," by R. Edmonds. *Educational Leadership,* October 1979, pp. 15–23.

   Search for Effective Schools: The Identification and Analysis of City Schools That Are Instructionally Effective for Poor Children, by R. Edmonds and J.R. Frederickson. (1978). Harvard University, Joint Center for Urban Studies.

35

Elementary and Secondary Education Act (ESEA)   See Improving America's Schools Act.

English as a Second Language (ESL)   Teaching English to non-English-speaking students in order for them to learn and succeed in U.S. schools. Because students who have limited English proficiency (LEP) must first acquire a greater ability to learn in the language to meet new academic standards, supplemental performance and assessment standards are needed while students gain mastery of English. Although there is debate concerning the effort and financing that U.S. schools should put into bilingual and ESL education, most research indicates these efforts are necessary for equitable education. The debate grows more intense among educators and legislators as demographics show growing numbers of non-English-speaking children in the United States. ESOL (English for Speakers of Other Languages) has generally the same meaning as ESL.

See also LEP (limited English proficiency) and Opportunity-to-Learn Standards.

enrichment   Topics and activities that are valuable and interesting to learn, but are not basic education. Knowledge that is "nice to know" but not necessarily what people "need to know." Examples might include study of Wordsworth's poetry or a biography of Alexander Hamilton, although people will not necessarily agree on what is basic and what is enrichment.

The term enrichment is also applied to efforts that parents make to supplement their children's learning outside of school, such as trips to science and art museums, educational vacations, visits to local libraries, and attendance at local theaters, orchestras, or ballets.

equal access   A term used in federal legislation (the Equal Access Act) that prohibits public school systems from discriminating against student religious groups. If schools permit other non-curriculum-related student groups, such as a chess club, to meet on school property, they must also permit other voluntary student groups, such as prayer groups, to meet.

36

Resource: *A Parent's Guide to Religion in the Public Schools.* Available from the Freedom Forum First Amendment Center, 1207 18th Ave. South, Nashville, TN 37212. Internet: http://www.fac.org

equity The goal of equity is to achieve a high-quality education with the same access to resources and with respect for all students, regardless of gender, race, ethnicity, socioeconomic status, disabilities, or special needs. All students should also be expected and encouraged to display academic excellence.

Studies show widespread inequities in tests, classroom expectations, texts and technological resources, and quality of teaching, especially in inner cities and among poor populations.

Resources: *Savage Inequalities,* by J. Kozol. Available from HarperCollins Publishers, 10 E. 53rd St., New York, NY 10022, tel. 800/242-7737.

Sex Bias in College Admissions Tests: Why Women Lose Out, by P. Rosser and FairTest Staff. Available from FairTest, 342 Broadway, Cambridge, MA 02139.

37

ESL See ENGLISH AS A SECOND LANGUAGE.

essential questions Questions derived from vitally important themes and topics whose answers cannot be summarized neatly and concisely. The essential questions and themes are a springboard to critical thinking and problem solving, and cause students to look at a subject in a different light and to consider and research new directions. Essential questions are often used to create units for INTERDISCIPLINARY STUDIES.

exemplar An example chosen to highlight characteristics of whatever it is an example of. The terms may refer to examples of student work used to show other students what they are expected to do. Such exemplars can also help teachers (and students themselves) evaluate student work. For example, a teacher might have students write a letter suitable for publication in the local newspaper commenting on a community issue. The teacher could provide RUBRICS specifying the criteria for evaluating the letters, along with sample letters written by previous students on a different topic at each level of quality (e.g., 4, 3, 2, 1 or A, B, C,D). Exemplars are sometimes called model papers.

exhibitions   Demanding projects designed and conducted by high school seniors in schools that are members of the COALITION OF ESSENTIAL SCHOOLS. Theodore Sizer, founder of the coalition, proposed the notion of exhibitions in his book *Horace's Compromise.* He recalled that students in 19th-century New England secondary schools were expected to present evidence of their learning as a requirement for graduation.

   Resources: *Graduation by Exhibition: Assessing Genuine Achievement,* by J. McDonald, E. Barton, S. Smith, D. Turner, and M. Finney. Available from ASCD, 1250 N. Pitt St., Alexandria, VA 22314-1453, tel. 703/549-9110, or 800/933-2723. Internet: http://www.ascd.org

   Horace's Compromise, The Dilemma of the American High School, by T. Sizer. Houghton Mifflin Co., One Beacon St., Boston, MA 02108, tel. 800/225-3362.

experiential education   Any form of education that emphasizes personal experience of the learner rather than learning from lectures, books, and other second-hand sources. The National Society for Experiential Education lists internships, service learning, school-to-work programs, field studies, cross-cultural education, leadership development, and ACTIVE LEARNING as varieties of experiential education.

   Resource: National Society for Experiential Education, 3509 Haworth Drive, Suite 207, Raleigh, NC 27609-7229.

experiential learning   See ACTIVE LEARNING.

38

Family Involvement Initiative   One of the eight current national education goals (also found in GOALS 2000) that calls for partnerships to increase parent involvement. To further this goal, the U.S. Department of Education has supported the National Coalition of Partners in Education (NCPIE), a group of more than 80 organizations that promote family involvement in children's learning, both in school and at home.

U.S. Secretary of Education Richard Riley has recommended seven family practices that encourage improved learning:

1. Find time to learn together.

2. Encourage children to reach their full potential by setting high (but realistic) standards and expectations.

3. Limit television viewing on school nights to two hours or less.

4. Read together.

5. Be sure that children take challenging courses and schedule daily time for homework. Provide a quiet environment and adequate time and space for homework.

6. Make sure children attend school every day, unless they are ill.

7. Be a good role model, and talk to children about values, as well as drugs and alcohol.

See also PARENT INVOLVEMENT and GOALS 2000.

Resources: *Developing Home-School Partnerships: From Concepts to Practice,* by S. Swap. New York: Teachers College Press.

The *Education Today Parent Involvement Handbook.* Available from the Educational Publishing Group, Suite 1215, 20 Park Plaza, Boston, MA 02116, tel. 617/542-6500, or 800/927-6006. Internet: http://www. familyeducation.com

How to Help Your Child with Homework: Every Caring Parent's Guide to Encouraging Good Study Habits and Ending the Homework Wars, by M. Radenich and J.S. Schumm. Available from Free Spirit Press, Suite 616, 400 First Avenue North, Minneapolis, MN 55401, tel. 612/338-2068, or 800/735-7323.

How to Involve Parents in a Multicultural School, by B. Davis. Available from ASCD, 1250 N. Pitt St., Alexandria, VA 22314-1453, tel. 703/549-9110, or 800/933-2723. Internet: http://www.ascd.org

The U.S. Department of Education has pamphlets on family involvement, 600 Independence Ave., SW, Washington, DC, tel. 800/USA-LEARN.

What's New in School: A Parents' Guide and *Involving Parents in School.* Videotape series. Available from ASCD, 1250 N. Pitt St., Alexandria, VA 22314-1453, tel. 703/549-9110, or 800/933-2723. Internet: http://www.ascd.org

40

family life education   School programs that teach the knowledge and attitudes needed by young people to become responsible members of healthy families, including essential attitudes and knowledge about human sexuality. Family life education programs are often controversial because one person's or group's idea about an essential attitude may be another person's or group's taboo.

flexible scheduling   Flexible scheduling, or modular scheduling, usually refers to school schedules in which classes are taught at different periods of time on various days. For the best effect, classes are also different sizes. For example, a lecture may be given to a large group for a relatively short time, but a seminar discussion would have fewer students for a longer class period. Flexible scheduling was tried by innovative secondary schools in the late 1960s and '70s, but few schools use it today. See also ALTERNATIVE SCHEDULING.

formative test   A test given primarily to determine what students have learned in order to plan further instruction. By contrast, an examination used primarily to document students' achievement at the end of a unit or course is considered a SUMMATIVE TEST.

full-service schools   See COMMUNITY CENTER SCHOOLS.

functional illiteracy   The inability to read or write well enough to perform many necessary tasks in life, such as writing a check, filling out a job application, reading a classified advertisement, or understanding a newspaper headline. Millions of people in the United States—some of whom are high school graduates—are functionally illiterate. A 1993 literacy survey found that one in five U.S. citizens cannot enter personal background information on a simple form.

Resources: International Reading Association, 800 Barksdale Road, P.O. Box 8139, Newark, DE 19714-8139, tel. 302/731-1600.

National Reading Styles Institute, P.O. Box 737, Syosset, NY 11791, tel. 800/331-3117.

Reading Is Fundamental (RIF), Suite 600, 600 Maryland Ave. SW, Washington, DC 20024, tel. 202/287-3220.

41

General Educational Development (GED) exam The GED exam is a high school equivalency test that was first developed in 1942. The American Council on Education regulates, standardizes, and norms the exam. Each year approximately 430,000 adults receive a GED diploma, certifying that they have skills and knowledge equivalent to those of a high school graduate.

The GED consists of five tests that cover writing skills, social studies, interpreting literature and the arts, science, and math; the tests can be taken individually or all at once. GED courses are often available in evening adult education programs in local school districts. The GED diploma is sometimes called an equivalency certificate.

Resources: American Council on Education, 2nd Floor, 1 Dupont Circle, Washington, D.C. 20036.

GED Hotline, tel. 800/626-9433.

gifted and talented The National Association for Gifted Children (NAGC) says "a gifted individual is someone who shows or has the potential for showing an exceptional level of ability in any one or a combination of various forms of expression." For example, a person may be exceptionally talented as an artist, a violinist, or a physicist.

In the past, giftedness has been measured by IQ tests, and people who scored in the upper two percent of the population were considered gifted. Some people measure giftedness or talent not by intelligence, but by consistently exceptional performance. The Education Consolidation and Improvement Act of 1981 refers to gifted and talented children as those who show high performance capability in specific academic fields or in areas such as creativity and leadership, and who require services or activities not ordinarily provided by the school to fully develop such capacity.

Resources: *Bringing Out the Best: A Resource Guide for Parents of Young Gifted Children,* by J. Saunders with P. Espeland. Available from Free Spirit Press, Suite 616, 400 First Avenue North, Minneapolis, MN 55401, tel. 612/338-2068, or 800/735-7323.

Challenging the Gifted in the Regular Classroom. Video and facilitator's manual. Available from ASCD, 1250 N. Pitt St., Alexandria, VA 22314-1453, tel. 703/549-9110, or 800/933-2723. Internet: http://www.ascd.org

How to Differentiate Instruction in Mixed-Ability Classrooms, by C.A. Tomlinson. Available from ASCD, 1250 N. Pitt St., Alexandria, VA 22314-1453, tel. 703/549-9110, or 800/933-2723. Internet www.ascd.org

TIDE: Talent Identification and Development in Education, by J. Feldhusen. Available from Center for Creative Learning, 4152 Independence Court, Sarasota, FL 34234-2147, tel. 941/351-8862.

43

goals   The expected end results of education as described by individual schools, districts, states, or other agencies. The U.S. Department of Education has supported development of voluntary national standards in a number of key areas, including science, social studies, and the arts. Other agencies have developed standards in other subjects, notably the National Council of Teachers of Mathematics (NCTM). Such statements of what schools are expected to accomplish and what students are expected to learn are sometimes called goals.

Goals 2000: Educate America Act   Signed into legislation on March 31, 1994, by President Clinton, and commonly called GOALS 2000, the act creates eight voluntary national goals as aspirations for U.S. schools. The legislation was set in motion at the 1989 National Education Summit by then-president George Bush. The eight goals specify that by the year 2000:

1. All children in the United States will start school ready to learn.

2. The high school graduation rate will increase to at least 90 percent.

3. All students will leave grades 4, 8, and 12 having demonstrated competence in challenging subject matter, including English, mathematics, science, foreign languages, civics and government, economics, the arts, history, and geography. Every school in the United States will ensure that all students learn to use their minds well so they may be prepared for responsible citizenship, further learning, and productive employment in the modern economy.

4. U.S. students will be the first in the world in mathematics and science achievement.

5. Every adult U.S. citizen will be literate and will possess the knowledge and skills necessary to compete in a global economy and exercise the rights and responsibilities of citizenship.

6. Every school in the United States will be free of drugs, violence, and the unauthorized presence of firearms and alcohol, and all will offer a disciplined learning environment conducive to learning.

7. The U.S. teaching force will have access to programs for the continued improvement of their professional skills and the opportunity to acquire the knowledge and skills needed to instruct and prepare all U.S. students for the next century.

8. Every school will promote partnerships that will increase parent involvement and participation in promoting the social, emotional, and academic growth of children.

States can apply for money by creating school improvement plans that address these goals. Nearly $500 million dollars will be spent for Goals 2000 in fiscal year 1997; $605 million was requested by President Clinton for fiscal year 1998.

See also SAFE SCHOOLS ACT and PARENT INVOLVEMENT.

Resources: Contact your state department of education, or call the National Goals Line at 800/USA-LEARN.

habits of mind   Mental attitudes and ways of behaving charac-   **45**
teristic of an educated person, such as being able to make a plan
and follow it, or making decisions based on sound information.
The habits of mind taught in ASCD's DIMENSIONS OF LEARNING program, for example, are grouped under the headings of critical
thinking, creative thinking, and self-regulated learning.

   Resource: *A Different Kind of Classroom: Teaching with Dimensions
of Learning,* by R.J. Marzano. Available from ASCD, 1250 N. Pitt St.,
Alexandria, VA   22314-1453, tel. 703/549-9110, or 800/933-2723.
Internet: http://www.ascd.org

Head Start   Since 1965, Head Start programs have been designed to provide a positive start in education for poor and
otherwise disadvantaged children ages 3 to 5 and their families.
The programs provide a range of services, including early childhood education, health and social services, parenting classes,
and nutritional information.

   About 90 percent of the families served by Head Start are at
or below the poverty level; about 10 percent of the children have
a disability. According to the Center for Workforce Preparation
and Quality Education, research indicates that participation in
Head Start and other early intervention programs makes it more
likely that the students will be literate, graduate high school, and

hold a job. The children who participate are also more likely to stay off welfare, avoid criminal activities, and attend college. Research shows that, for each AT-RISK child, spending $4,800 to support and encourage the child's education would save society $29,000 in welfare, social services, and legal costs.

Resources: The Center for Workforce Preparation and Quality Education, 1615 H St. NW, Washington, DC 20062.

National Head Start Association, 1651 Prince St., Alexandria, VA 22314, tel. 703/739-0875.

heterogeneous grouping (mixed grouping)   The opposite of HOMOGENEOUS GROUPING, heterogeneous grouping intentionally mixes students of varying talents and needs so they can learn, help, and respect one another as individuals, and appreciate each person's unique set of abilities. The success of this method of grouping depends on the teacher's skill in managing and supporting students, and ensuring that every student is involved and needed in group tasks.

A group studying the ocean, for example, may include a child who likes math to calculate depths, one who is artistic to illustrate the ocean at various depths, a mildly autistic child who enjoys doing research to find some needed details, and a child with good penmanship or keyboarding skills to finalize the report. All of the children boost their self-esteem because each becomes a valued, contributing team member, and each can serve as a tutor to the others in a particular area of expertise.

Opponents of heterogeneous grouping say that it may develop social skills among the group members, but it hampers the brightest children from moving at an accelerated pace. They also argue that heterogeneous grouping waters down the curriculum for all the students.

Resources: Crossing the Tracks: How 'Untracking' Can Save America's Schools, by A. Wheelock. Available from W.W. Norton & Co., 500 Fifth Ave., New York, NY 10110, tel. 800/233-4830.

Educating Everybody's Children: Diverse Teaching Strategies for Diverse Learners, edited by R.W. Cole. Available from ASCD, 1250 N. Pitt St., Alexandria, VA 22314-1453, tel. 703/549-9110, or 800/933-2723. Internet: http://www.ascd.org

How to Differentiate Instruction in Mixed-Ability Classrooms, by C.A. Tomlinson. Available from ASCD, 1250 N. Pitt St., Alexandria, VA 22314-1453, tel. 703/549-9110, or 800/933-2723. Internet: http://www. ascd. org

46

How to Untrack Your School, by P. George. Available from ASCD, 1250 N. Pitt St., Alexandria, VA 22314-1453, tel. 703/549-9110, or 800/933-2723. Internet: http://www.ascd.org

higher-order thinking skills   Higher-order thinking, or complex reasoning, asks students to go beyond the basic skill of memorizing information by developing their ability to process information and apply it to a variety of situations. The mental processes involved include analyzing, comparing, contrasting, generalizing, problem solving, investigating, experimenting, and creating. New methods of teaching and assessing, such as BRAIN-BASED LEARNING, PERFORMANCE ASSESSMENTS, COOPERATIVE LEARNING, and AUTHENTIC LEARNING are intended to develop higher-order thinking skills.

Other terms used to refer to higher-order thinking skills include critical thinking, complex reasoning, and thinking skills.

Resources: *Developing Minds,* by A. Costa. Two volumes. Available from ASCD, 1250 N. Pitt St., Alexandria, VA 22314-1453, tel. 703/549-9110, or 800/933-2723. Internet: http://www.ascd.org

Readings from Educational Leadership: Teaching Thinking, edited by R.S. Brandt. Available from ASCD, 1250 N. Pitt St., Alexandria, VA 22314-1453, tel. 703/549-9110, or 800/933-2723. Internet: http://www.ascd.org

47

holistic learning   A theory of education that places importance on the complete experience of learning and the ways in which the separate parts of the learning experience are interrelated. Canadian scholar John Miller defines it as "essentially concerned with connections in human experience," such as the connections between mind and body, rational thought and intuition, various subject matter, and the individual in society. Teaching methods that complement this type of learning include INTERDISCIPLINARY CURRICULUM, MULTICULTURAL EDUCATION, and WHOLE LANGUAGE reading programs.

Resources: *The Holistic Curriculum,* by J. Miller. Toronto, Ont.: OISE Press, Ontario Institute for Studies in Education.

Holistic Education Review. Available quarterly from Holistic Education Press, P.O. Box 328, Brandon, VT 05733-0328, tel. 800/639-4122. E-mail: holistic@sover.net. Internet: http://www.sover.net/~holistic/

home schooling An education option in which families teach their children at home instead of sending them to public or private schools. Requirements vary from state to state; some require a home-schooling parent to have a teaching degree. In the mid-1980s about 15,000 home schools existed, but by 1995 the U.S. Department of Education reported more than 350,000.

Families choose home schooling for a variety of reasons, often religious differences with public education or dissatisfaction with the quality of public education. Families are beginning to network their home-schooling efforts with other families to create COOPERATIVE LEARNING situations and opportunities for field trips. In some states, home schools and public schools are working together to benefit all the students. For example, home-schooled teens in Reinhardt, Texas, tutor public elementary school students. Also, home-schooled children in Iowa can enroll in public schools for academic and extracurricular programs.

48

Most home-schooled students must take tests to show what they have learned, especially if they apply for admission to institutes of higher education.

Resources: Educational Leadership, September 1994. Theme issue on "The New Alternative Schools."

Home Schooling: The Educational Alternative magazine. Circulation Department, 470 Boston Post Road, Weston, MA 02193, tel. 617/899-2702.

homogeneous grouping Also called tracking or ability grouping, this method organizes children according to their displayed abilities and aptitudes. For example, college-bound students might have all of their classes together while vocational students and special education students might attend their own classes.

A variation of ability grouping places students according to their abilities in the subject. For example, students may be placed in above-average science courses and average English courses, or vice versa, to fit their aptitudes in the subjects.

Proponents of ability grouping believe it allows students to excel within their levels, and say that less capable students need not be intimidated by their more capable peers, and that gifted students need not be bored by the slower pace often believed to be necessary for other students. Ability grouping is frequently found in school settings where traditional teaching methods (e.g., lecture and recitation) are also used.

Critics say this kind of tracking is undemocratic, allows unequal access to higher-level content, and creates low self-esteem. Opponents also say that students who learn more slowly or who need alternative teaching styles become victims of lower performance expectations. They argue that remedial work does not promote a love of learning.

See also AT-RISK and HETEROGENEOUS GROUPING.

immersion   In immersion bilingual education programs, students learn a second language by speaking, hearing, and reading it all day (or for part of the day), including being taught several subjects in that language. In most cases the lessons are constructed around the students' language competencies, and the instructor is fluent in both the students' language and the language being learned. Immersion programs in the United States are usually for non-English speakers, but some enrichment immersion programs are designed for English speakers to learn a second language.

Improving America's Schools Act (IASA)   Formerly called the Elementary and Secondary Education Act, the IASA is directed at improving education primarily for America's poor and disadvantaged students.

IASA also emphasizes the PROFESSIONAL DEVELOPMENT of teachers, principals, and other school staff members to enable them to help all students, including those with special needs, to reach high standards. In addition, it supports the development of CHARTER SCHOOLS.

IASA programs target linguistically and culturally diverse students, children's multiple intelligences, and students with learning difficulties. IASA includes Title I and the Safe and Drug-Free Schools and Communities Act.

Resource: The U.S. Department of Education, 600 Independence Ave., SW, Washington, DC, 20202, tel. 800/USA-LEARN.

inclusion and full inclusion The practice of educating all or most children in the same classroom, including children with physical, mental, and developmental disabilities. Inclusion classes often require a special assistant to the classroom teacher.

In a fully inclusive school or classroom, all of the children follow the same schedules; everyone is involved in the same field trips, extracurricular activities, and assemblies. All of the children use the same facilities. To be inclusive, classrooms must be RESTRUCTURED to support each child. Children in inclusive classrooms can take advantage of COOPERATIVE LEARNING, CURRICULUM adaptations, classroom aides, environmental accommodations, cooperation between regular and special education teachers, proactive behavior plans, and peer tutoring.

51

The 1975 Education for All Handicapped Children Act (P.L. 94-142) made inclusion a controversial topic by requiring a free and appropriate education with related services for each child in the least restrictive environment possible, and an INDIVIDUALIZED EDUCATION PROGRAM (IEP) for each qualifying child. In 1991 the bill was renamed the INDIVIDUALS WITH DISABILITIES EDUCATION ACT (IDEA) and the revision broadened the definition of disabilities and added related services.

One controversy involves interpreting the phrase "least restrictive environment possible." Supporters of full inclusion interpret this phrase to mean full provisions in the regular school; others advocate case-by-case decisions, considering the individual student and available staff and facilities. For example, some professionals and some parents of children with learning disabilities believe that these children benefit from partial inclusion, with some activities and learning experiences occurring in alternative facilities using different teaching strategies. The official policy statement of the Learning Disabilities Association of America—a nonprofit organization of parents, professionals, and people with learning disabilities—opposes full inclusion.

Inclusion has passionate advocates and adversaries. Opponents, including many parents of children with special needs, feel that the presence of many children with disabilities holds back average and gifted students and that SPECIAL-NEEDS students are frequently disruptive and are not well served by inclusion. Advocates of inclusion present evidence that all students are better served in structured inclusive classrooms—that children with disabilities receive more understanding and respect from their peers and that all students are able to learn more by working together.

Resources: *Creating an Inclusive School,* edited by R.A.Villa and J.S. Thousand. Available from ASCD, 1250 N. Pitt St., Alexandria, VA 22314-1453, tel. 703/549-9110, or 800/933-2723. Internet: http://www.ascd.org

Inclusion. Video series. Available from ASCD, 1250 N. Pitt St., Alexandria, VA 22314-1453, tel. 703/549-9110, or 800/933-2723. Internet: http://www.ascd.org

The National Center for Children and Youth with Disabilities, P.O. Box 1492, Washington, DC 20013-1492, tel. 800/695-0285 (Voice/TT).

Support Networks for Inclusive Schooling: Interdependent Integrated Education, edited by W. Stainback and S. Stainback. Baltimore, Md.: P.H. Brookes Pub. Co.

indicator A statistic, such as percentage of students attending school daily, used as evidence of success in accomplishing an abstract goal, such as student interest in learning. The long-term results of education are difficult to measure, so people use measurable indicators, such as drop-out rates, honors won, and test scores, to help judge school quality.

individual education accounts (William D. Ford Federal Direct Loan Program) IEAs are intended to make college available, affordable, and manageable for families. The following basic ideas are behind individual education accounts:

- Borrowers can receive loans directly through their schools, thus eliminating the confusing system of banks, guaranty agencies, secondary markets, and loan services.
- Fees and interest rates are lowered, saving borrowers significant money.
- Borrowers choose a repayment plan, allowing them to match payments with their ability to pay.

- Borrowers can refinance existing student loans to consolidate their payments.

Resources: The *Education Today College Guide* contains information on college financing, as well as other information for parents, students, and high school counselors. Available from the Educational Publishing Group, 20 Park Plaza, Suite 1215, Boston, MA 02116, tel. 617/542-6500, or 800/927-6006, ext. 127. Internet: http://www.familyeducation.com

The Student Guide: Financial Aid from the Department of Education. Available from the Federal Student Aid Information Center, P.O. Box 84, Washington, DC 20044-0084.

individualized education   The practice of giving lessons and assignments according to each student's needs and strengths. Students work at their own pace, eliminating the problem of students falling behind or becoming bored. See also CONTINUOUS PROGRESS.

individualized education program (IEP)   Students with certain special needs, as specified by the INDIVIDUALS WITH DISABILITIES EDUCATION ACT (IDEA), have a legal right to a unique plan of education written by a multidisciplinary team. After a series of tests and observations determine the child's need for an IEP, a team (generally including a special education teacher, a classroom teacher, a building principal, a psychologist, and the child's parents or guardians) designs a program of services to blend the best methods of teaching with the most conducive learning environment for the child.

The process of creating the IEP allows the parties to discuss and resolve any differences of opinions and needs. The document specifies the decisions and anticipated outcomes, and includes the child's current level of educational performance, specific services to be provided (and provider), anticipated time periods when these special services will be provided, the amount of time the child will be in regular and in special classrooms, along with short- and long-term goals. The IEP objectives are used to determine the child's progress toward the goals.

A well-written, carefully developed IEP protects the child because schools are legally responsible for implementing it.

Resources: The Coordinating Council for Handicapped Children has posted "How to Participate in Your Child's IEP Meeting" on the World Wide Web at http://services.bunip.com:2331/lawoffic/aiiep.html.

Request briefing paper from the National Information Center for Children and Youth with Disabilities (LG2, Update March 1994) by writing to NICCHY, P.O. Box 1492, Washington, DC 20013-1492, tel. 202/884-8200.

Individuals with Disabilities Education Act (IDEA, P.L. 101-476) An amendment to the Education for All Handicapped Children Act (P.L. 94- 142), the IDEA is a federal law passed in 1991 that guarantees a free and appropriate education for eligible children and youth with disabilities.

The language of the law defines a specific learning disability as "a disorder in one or more of the basic psychological processes involved in undertaking or using language, spoken or written, which may manifest itself in an imperfect ability to listen, think, read, write, spell, or to do mathematical calculations." Children not included under this law include those who "have learning problems which are primarily the result of visual, hearing, or other hardships, of mental retardation, of emotional disturbance, or of environmental, cultural, or economic disadvantage."

Resource: Learning Disabilities and the Law, by P.S. Latham and P.H. Latham. Washington, D.C.: JKL Communications.

information superhighway See INTERNET.

integrated language arts A way of teaching phonics, grammar, handwriting, spelling, and other language skills together rather than as separate subjects. Students spend their instructional time reading, writing, listening, and speaking; teachers help them learn skills naturally, as they are needed. Critics contend that students may miss important information and skills without systematic instruction. Proponents of integrated language arts say that teaching skills in context is more interesting and meaningful to students and therefore more effective.

integrated learning systems Computer-based systems that provide interactive instruction to individual students and

54

maintain records of each student's progress. Sophisticated systems adapt the level of instruction to the student's achievement, giving slower students additional help and moving successful students to more challenging levels.

interactive learning Occurs when the source of instruction communicates directly with the learner, shaping responses to the learner's needs. Tutoring—one teacher teaching a single student—is highly interactive. Computers and other modern technological applications have made it theoretically possible to provide effective interactive instruction to any learner on any subject.

interdisciplinary curriculum A philosophy of teaching in which content is drawn from several subject areas to focus on a particular topic or theme. Rather than studying math or social studies in isolation, for example, a class might study a unit called The Sea, using math to calculate pressure at certain depths and social studies to understand why coastal and inland populations have different livelihoods.

55

Effective interdisciplinary studies include the following elements:

- A topic that lends itself to study from several points of view.
- Two to five valuable themes (or ESSENTIAL QUESTIONS) the teacher wants the students to explore.
- An approach and activities to further students' understanding more than is possible in a traditional, single-discipline unit.

Resources: *Integrating the Curriculum.* Videos, facilitator's guide, and book. Available from ASCD, 1250 N. Pitt St., Alexandria, VA 22314-1453, tel. 703/549-9110, or 800/933-2723. Internet: http://www.ascd. org

Interdisciplinary Curriculum: Design and Implementation, by H.H. Jacobs. Available from ASCD, 1250 N. Pitt St., Alexandria, VA 22314-1453, tel. 703/549-9110, or 800/933-2723. Internet: http:// www.ascd.org

Planning the Integrated Curriculum: The Call to Adventure, by S. Drake. Available from ASCD, 1250 N. Pitt St., Alexandria, VA 22314-1453, tel. 703/549-9110, 800/933-2723. Internet: http://www.ascd.org

international baccalaureate (IB) A rigorous, pre-university course of study that leads to examinations accepted by more than 70 countries for university admission. Candidates for IB diplomas study languages, sciences, mathematics, and humanities in the final two years of secondary schooling. The program is a compromise between the countries that call for specialization of knowledge and those that prefer breadth of knowledge.

The idea for an IB grew from concerns of schools that had to prepare students to take university entrance exams around the world. In 1962 the International Schools Association began to explore the creation of an international standard exam, and by 1970 the first exam was offered to 20 schools. The IB is now offered by more than 500 schools. Schools must meet certain criteria to offer IB curriculum and to administer the exam. Students cannot take the IB unless they are enrolled in an authorized school.

The headquarters of the International Baccalaureate Organization is located in Geneva, Switzerland, but the IBO also maintains regional offices around the world.

Resource: International Baccalaureate/North America, Suite 2007, 200 Madison Ave., New York, NY 10016, tel. 212/696-4464, fax 212/889-9242.

Internet The network of computer networks, the Internet is a worldwide information and communications system available to people with access to a computer, modem, and Internet service provider (ISP). The Internet includes encyclopedias, books, newspapers, researchers, teachers, associations, college courses, collectors' clubs, electronic mail, online chat groups, news groups, and bulletin boards.

Schools use online services to link their classes with various educational programs around the world. One example is Ocean Challenge, which allows students in classrooms to follow a Canadian-based semester-at-sea program, Class Afloat. The program is interdisciplinary because students study the ocean while learning about marine life, astronomy, weather, physics, social studies, geography, and languages. (See also INTERDISCIPLINARY CURRICULUM.)

Other terms associated with the Internet include the Net, information superhighway, and the World Wide Web (WWW).

Several commercial services make navigating or finding what you want in the maze of information somewhat easier.

Resources: *Educator's Internet Companion,* by Classroom Connect. Available from Classroom Connect-Prentice Hall, Upper Saddle River, N.J. 07458, tel. 201/236-7000.

Everything You Need to Know (But Were Afraid to Ask Kids) About the Information Highway, by M. Marsh. Available from the Computer Learning Foundation, P.O. Box 60007, Palo Alto, CA 94306, tel. 415/327-3347.

Ocean Challenge, 20 Park Plaza, Suite 424, Boston, MA 02116, tel. 617/357-0055.

Teaching & Learning with the Internet. Facilitator's guide and two videotapes. Available from ASCD, 1250 N. Pitt St., Alexandria, VA 22314-1453, tel. 703/549-9110, or 800/933-2723. Internet: http://www.ascd.org

Way of the Ferret: Finding Educational Resources on the Internet, by T. LaQuey. Available from Addison-Wesley Publishing Co., Route 128, Reading, MA 01867, tel. 800/638-3030.

The Whole Internet User's Guide & Catalog, 2nd ed., by E. Krol. Available from O'Reilly & Associates, Sebastopol, CA. *The Whole Internet Catalog* is on the World Wide Web at http://gnn.comgnn/wic/index.html.

lead teachers　Teachers who have broader responsibilities and higher salaries than other teachers, but continue to work with students as regular classroom teachers, at least part time. The idea for lead teachers was proposed as a way to improve the quality of schooling in 1986 in a report from a task force that included leaders of both major teacher unions. The task force noted that education is different from most professions in that opportunities for career advancement are relatively limited. Despite various efforts to improve the status and rewards of teaching, few of today's teachers hold positions that could be considered lead teacher roles.

Resource: *A Nation Prepared: Teachers for the 21st Century* (1986). Available from the Carnegie Forum on Education and the Economy, P.O. Box 157, Hyattsville, MD 20781.

learning disability (LD)　A condition that interferes with a student's ability to learn. Even the definition of this term is controversial. The language provided in the law to protect learning-disabled students excludes students with problems such as ATTENTION DEFICIT (HYPERACTIVITY) DISORDER. A definition created by the National Joint Commission for Learning Disabilities adds that "problems in self-regulatory behavior, social perception, and social interaction" may occur in persons with LD, but those behaviors are not to be considered learning disabilities in themselves.

The characteristics of LD are numerous and may include problems in the following areas:

- Fine and gross motor skills.
- Hearing and visual perceptions (such as seeing letters or numbers in reverse).
- Staying on task and paying attention (ADD related).
- Linguistic processing and expression.
- Social skills.
- Emotional distress.

The exact causes of LD are generally unknown, but theories include defects in the central nervous system and genetic mutations. See also INDIVIDUALS WITH DISABILITIES EDUCATION ACT.

Resources: Council for Learning Disabilities, P.O. Box 40303, Overland Park, KS 66204, tel. 913/492-8755.

Keys to Parenting a Child with a Learning Disability, by B.E. McNamara and F.J. McNamara. Available from Barron's Educational Series, 250 Wireless Blvd., Hauppauge, NY 11788, tel. 516/434-3311, or 800/645-3476.

Learning Disability Association of America, 4156 Library Road, Pittsburgh, PA 15234, tel. 412/341-1515.

learning disorder A physical or psychological disability that interferes with a student's ability to learn. For example, some people have a condition known as DYSLEXIA, which simply means a reading disability. People with this condition cannot distinguish among letters of the alphabet or translate words on paper into meaningful language as easily as most other people.

learning styles Descriptions of learning styles are attempts to define and accommodate the way in which a student learns most readily. All children can learn, but each person concentrates, processes, and absorbs new information differently. According to Rita Dunn, some 21 elements of learning style affect student achievement and motivation.

People think and learn in many different ways. When students perform poorly in a subject it is often because of the way they were taught and not their inability to learn. According to

Robert Sternberg, "Teachers and students alike confuse mismatches in styles of teaching and learning with lack of ability."

Research indicates that teaching underachievers in ways that complement their strengths can significantly increase their scores on standardized tests. For example, strongly auditory students learn and recall information when they hear it, whereas kinesthetic youngsters need to physically experience what they are to learn through activities such as role playing or floor games.

To make the most of research in this area, teachers need to broaden their methods of teaching to reach students. TEAM TEACHING is another valuable alternative, because teachers use different teaching styles.

Resources: "Allowing for Styles of Thinking," by R.J. Sternberg. *Educational Leadership*, November 1994, pp. 36–40.

Cognitive Type Theory & Learning Style, by Carolyn Mamchur. (1996). Available from ASCD, 1250 N. Pitt St., Alexandria, VA 22314-1453, tel. 703/549-9110, or 800/933-2723. Internet: http://www.ascd. org

Educating Everybody's Children: Diverse Teaching Strategies for Diverse Learners, edited by R.W. Cole. Available from ASCD, 1250 N. Pitt St., Alexandria, VA 22314-1453, tel. 703/549-9110, or 800/933-2723. Internet: http://www.ascd.org

How to Implement and Supervise a Learning Style Program, by Rita Dunn. (1996). Available from ASCD, 1250 N. Pitt St., Alexandria, VA 22314-1453, tel. 703/549-9110, or 800/933-2723. Internet: http://www. ascd.org

"Reading Styles: High Gains for the Bottom Third," by M. Carbo. *Educational Leadership*, February 1996, pp. 8–13.

Teaching to Learning Styles. Video, book, and manual. Available from ASCD, 1250 N. Pitt St., Alexandria, VA 22314-1453, tel. 703/549-9110, or 800/933-2723. Internet: http://www.ascd.org

LEP (Limited English Proficiency)   Students who have not yet achieved mastery in reading, writing, listening, or speaking English but are fluent in another language have limited English proficiency (LEP). These students need access to BILINGUAL EDUCATION or ENGLISH AS A SECOND LANGUAGE (ESL) classes to gain proficiency in English. See also OPPORTUNITY-TO-LEARN STANDARDS.

looping   An informal term for assigning students to the same teacher for more than one school year. Rather than teaching a new group of students at the same grade level each year, teachers stay with the same group of students as they move from grade to grade, then "loop" back after two or more years to start again with a new group. Looping is rare in the United States, but is common in some parts of Europe and becoming more popular in the United States. Advocates say it helps teachers know their students and provides for more continuous learning.

magnet schools   Specialized public schools that usually focus on a particular area of study, such as the arts or science and technology, as well as offering regular school subjects. Magnet schools may also subscribe to a particular philosophy of learning, such as back-to-basics or multicultural education. Magnet schools must meet local and state requirements in such areas as curriculum, hiring, and diversity of the student body.

Magnet schools are considered alternatives to the regular public schools in the district. Students throughout the school district may enroll and the schools often have waiting lists. Some magnet schools have specific entry requirements, such as proven aptitudes for the area of concentration at the school, but other magnets do not. Most magnet schools were established in large urban school districts to help achieve racial desegregation.

Many families find magnet schools attractive because of their strong pedagogical base. In addition, the coherence that is provided by the school's focused program gives students a sense of direction and aids in their career preparation. (See PEDAGOGY.)

Teachers and administrators at magnet schools are often committed to the school philosophy, as are the students and their families. A strong sense of community results, and thus the SCHOOL CLIMATE is usually orderly, safe, and nurturing. In addition, magnet schools frequently employ reform strategies such as HETEROGENEOUS GROUPING and COOPERATIVE LEARNING, and have a high level of parent involvement. See also ALTERNATIVE SCHOOLS.

Resource: Magnet Schools: Recent Developments and Perspectives, edited by N. Estes, D.U. Levine, and D.R. Waldrip. Morgan Printing and Publishing, Suite 135, 900 Old Koenig Lane, Austin, TX 78756, tel. 512/459-5194.

mainstreaming The practice of placing students with LEARNING DISABILITIES or other SPECIAL NEEDS into regular classrooms. Mainstreaming differs from INCLUSION by assuming that students with special needs will be provided with additional assistance and instruction outside the regular classroom (often in the RESOURCE ROOM). Mainstreaming is also known as partial inclusion.

Successful mainstreaming occurs when there is regular communication and cooperation among teachers, students, and parents. INDIVIDUALIZED EDUCATION PROGRAMS need to be jointly developed, thoroughly understood, and carefully followed. The classroom teacher may need special training and assistance from the special education staff.

Mainstreaming is more effective when non-disabled students are given information about their peers with special needs.

Resources: Lessons Learned: Students with Learning Disabilities Share What They've Learned about Life and Learning, by D. Fullen. Available from Amazon.com. Internet: http://www.amazon.com

manipulatives Learning materials that students can work with physically to give them the opportunity to understand abstract ideas by using concrete objects. An abacus is a math manipulative.

mastery learning A way of organizing instruction that tries to make sure students have mastered each increment of a subject before going on to the next. The idea assumes that a subject can be subdivided into sequential steps organized hierarchically. The classic mastery learning model formulated by psychologist Benjamin Bloom calls for teachers to teach a unit of work and give a FORMATIVE TEST. Students who do not master the material study it in a different way while the mastery students do ENRICHMENT work and may tutor their nonmastery peers. Then all stu-

63

dents take a SUMMATIVE TEST, which nearly all students are expected to pass.

mediation   Professional mediation is often the recourse taken by school boards when teacher contract negotiations halt. Mediation over contract specifications is binding arbitration in some states, meaning that the board and union must accept the terms negotiated.

In other situations involving CONFLICT RESOLUTION, a mediator is a neutral party who works between the two conflicting parties and attempts to arrive at a satisfactory compromise.

mentor   A mentor is a role model who offers support to another person. A mentor has knowledge and experience in an area and shares it with the person being mentored. For example, an experienced teacher might mentor a student teacher or beginning teacher.

64

Some mentoring programs are designed to keep AT-RISK students in school. Acting as role models, mentors spend time with individual students once or twice a week—encouraging, listening, making suggestions, and taking the student to events, activities, or to the mentor's place of employment to help the student learn about a career and consider further education.

Resources: How to Mentor in the Midst of Change, by C. Granade Sullivan. Available from ASCD, 1250 N. Pitt St., Alexandria, VA 22314-1453, tel. 703/549-9110, or 800/933-2723. Internet: http://www.ascd.org

Mentoring the New Teacher, videotape series, produced by J.B. Rawley and P.M. Hart of the University of Dayton, Ohio. Available from ASCD, 1250 N. Pitt St., Alexandria, VA 22314-1453, tel. 703/549-9110, or 800/933-2723. Internet: http://www.ascd.org

Resource Manual for Campus-Based Youth Mentoring Programs. Available from Education Commission of the States, Suite 2700, 707 17th St., Denver, CO 80202-3427, tel. 303/299-3692.

merit pay   An approach to rewarding exemplary teachers by paying them higher salaries based on their performance or the performance of their students. Merit pay is controversial because the grounds for awarding it tend to be subjective. Because students learn in different ways and teachers teach with different styles, many people believe that it is unfair to regard one teacher as better than another.

Most educators do not consider merit pay, by itself, an effective means of improving teacher performance. Some school districts have combined merit pay with other factors—such as additional planning time, training, flexible assignments, and changes in working conditions or environments—and they report that the distinctions have helped them retain high-quality teachers.

metacognition   The ability to be conscious of and, to some degree, control one's own thinking. The prefix "meta" has come to be used by educators to refer to thinking about "the thing itself." In this case, cognition is thinking, so metacognition means thinking about one's own thinking.

You are using metacognition when you track where you are in solving a multistep problem or when you realize that you have been looking at a page in a book without following the meaning and backtrack until you find the place where your mind began to wander.

65

middle schools   Schools for students in the early adolescent years between elementary school and high school. Most middle schools include grades 5 through 8 or 6 through 8. Middle school advocates say that young adolescents have special needs because of their rapid growth and change. They say middle schools should have TEAM TEACHING, INTERDISCIPLINARY CURRICULUM, ADVISORY SYSTEMS, and other provisions for PERSONALIZATION. Junior high schools, which have traditionally included grades 7–9, do not usually have these features.

Resources: *The Middle School—and Beyond,* by P. George, C. Stevenson, J. Thomason, and J. Beane. Available from ASCD, 1250 N. Pitt St., Alexandria, VA 22314-1453, tel. 703/549-9110, or 800/933-2723. Internet: http://www.ascd.org

Teaching Ten- to Fourteen-Year-Olds, by C. Stevenson. White Plains, N.Y.: Longman.

Transforming Middle Schools: A Guide to Whole-School Change, by B. Raebeck. Lancaster, Pa.: Technomic Pub. Co.

mixed grouping   See HETEROGENEOUS GROUPING.

multi-age grouping   The practice of having children of different ages in the same classroom, rather than assigning children to classrooms by their age (e.g., 6-year-old children to 1st grade and 7-year-old children to 2nd grade). Multi-age grouping is practiced more often in elementary schools than in secondary schools. A typical grouping is children ages 5–7 as primary students and children ages 8–10 as intermediate students. The reason for blending two or more grade levels is to improve learning, but teacher training and preparation are necessary to ensure its success.

Resources: "A Basic Understanding of Multi-age Grouping," by B.A. Miller. *The School Administrator,* January 1996, pp. 12–17.

Exploring the Multi-age Classroom, by A. Bingham, P. Dorta, M. McClaskey, and J. O'Keefe. York, Me.: Stenhouse.

"The Results of Multi-age Grouping," by D. Jeanroy. *The School Administrator,* January 1996, pp. 18–19.

66   **multicultural education**   Schooling that helps students understand and relate to cultural, ethnic, and other diversity. Gwendolyn Baker, former head of the U.S. Committee for UNICEF and an expert on multicultural education and curriculum development, defines multicultural education as a process through which individuals are exposed to the diversity within the United States and throughout the world. Cultural groups are defined not only by ethnicity and race, but also by religion, language, gender, socioeconomics, age, and mental and physical differences.

Multiculturalism should be a process that encourages people to work together and to celebrate differences, not to be separated by them. Some multiculturalists believe that focusing on a student's own culture is a natural first step to widening the student's perspectives. Other advocates believe that emphasizing the differences between groups promotes fragmentation and rivalries. They see multicultural education as a process that allows and encourages teachers to integrate various cultures' beliefs, music, language, and social skills into each school subject, as appropriate.

Opponents of multicultural education feel that it detracts from students' understanding of traditional beliefs and history. Supporters feel that multicultural education provides a more balanced look at history and the world, and that studying several viewpoints increases students' depth of understanding.

Resources: Educating Everybody's Children: Diverse Teaching Strategies for Diverse Learners, edited by R.W. Cole. Available from ASCD, 1250 N. Pitt St., Alexandria, VA 22314-1453, tel. 703/549-9110, or 800/933-2723. Internet: http://www.ascd.org

The Evolving Multicultural Classroom, by R. Reissman. Available from ASCD, 1250 N. Pitt St., Alexandria, VA 22314-1453, tel. 703/549-9110, or 800/933-2723. Internet: http://www.ascd.org

Multicultural Education. Videotape series. Available from ASCD, 1250 N. Pitt St., Alexandria, VA 22314-1453, tel. 703/549-9110, or 800/933-2723. Internet: http://www.ascd.org

Multicultural Education: Issues and Perspectives, by J.A. Banks, 3rd ed., Boston: Allyn & Bacon, Inc., Division of Simon & Schuster Higher Education Group, 160 Gould St., Needham Heights, MA 02194.

Planning and Organizing for Multicultural Instruction, by G. Baker. Available from Addison-Wesley Publishing Co., Route 128, Reading, MA 01867, tel. 800/447-2226.

67

multidisciplinary curriculum   One of several terms that refer to curriculum in more than one discipline, or subject area. People may use these terms differently, but in general, a multidisciplinary curriculum is one in which the same topic, for example, harmony, is studied from the viewpoint of more than one discipline (e.g., music, history, and literature). Each subject is taught separately, but the two subjects are intentionally related to the same topic. An INTERDISCIPLINARY curriculum implies that the topic is studied as a whole, but from the perspective of several disciplines. Strictly speaking, integrated curriculum involves study of topics without regard to any particular academic disciplines.

multimedia presentations   Presentations that use more than one medium (such as auditory and visual information) to teach topics. Multimedia presentations are used both by teachers to cover new subject matter and by students to present projects.

The term also is applied to the combination of text, pictures, sound, voice, animation, and video that make up a CD-ROM.

multiple intelligences   Refers to a theory of intelligence developed in the mid-1980s by Howard Gardner, professor of education at Harvard University. Gardner defines intelligence as "the ability to solve problems or fashion products that are valued in at least one culture." IQ tests, he points out, cannot measure the value of a product or one's ability to produce a product.

Gardner originally identified seven intelligences: linguistic, logical-mathematical, musical, spatial, bodily-kinesthetic, interpersonal, and intrapersonal. He now suggests the existence of several others, including naturalist, spiritual, and existential. Everyone has these intelligences in different proportions. Teachers who use multiple intelligences theories strive to present subject matter in ways that use language, numbers, physical surroundings, sound, the body, and social skills.

Resources: "Are There Additional Intelligences? The Case for Naturalist, Spiritual, and Existential Intelligences," by H. Gardner. (1996). In *Education, Information and Transformation*, edited by J. Kane. Available from Prentice-Hall, Upper Saddle River, N.J. 07458, tel. 201/ 236-7000.

Frames of Mind and *The Unschooled Mind*, both by H. Gardner. Available from Basic Books, 10 E. 53rd St., New York, NY 10022, tel. 800/ 638-3030.

Multiple Intelligences in the Classroom, by T. Armstrong. Available from ASCD, 1250 N. Pitt St., Alexandria, VA 22314-1453, tel. 703/549-9110, or 800/933-2723. Internet: http://www.ascd.org

The Multiple Intelligences Series. Videos, guides, and books. Available from ASCD, 1250 N. Pitt St., Alexandria, VA 22314-1453, tel. 703/549-9110, or 800/933-2723. Internet: http://www.ascd.org

"Reflections on Multiple Intelligences: Myths and Messages," by H. Gardner. *Phi Delta Kappan*, November 1995, pp. 200–209.

n

National and Community Service Trust Act See AMERICORPS.

National Assessment of Educational Progress, or NAEP (pronounced "nape"), is also known as The Nation's Report Card. It is a federally funded program (currently contracted to Educational Testing Service, Princeton, N.J.) which provides information about the achievement of U.S. students nationally and state-by-state. NAEP tests a representative sample of students in grades 4, 8, and 12 each year and reports the results to the public.

National Board for Professional Teaching Standards (NBPTS) The organization creating a series of comprehensive assessments that teachers may take voluntarily to become nationally certified as outstanding teachers. (Regular certification is at the state level.) NBPTS President James Kelly says, "The assessment process validated by the National Board goes far beyond the traditional pencil-and-paper exams to measure fully the breadth and depth of a teacher's expertise."

NBPTS board members are mostly teachers. The Board's mission is to "establish high and rigorous standards for what accomplished teachers should know and be able to do, to . . . assess and certify teachers who meet these standards, and to advance related education reforms that improve learning in American schools."

Resource: Contact the NBPTS, Suite 400, 26555 Evergreen Road, Southfield, MI 48076, tel. 810/351-4444, or 800/22-TEACH.

New American Schools Development Corporation

Launched in 1991, NASDC is a nonprofit, nonpartisan organization supported by U.S. corporations, foundations, and individuals. It seeks to "develop innovative schools that address the learning needs of all children, establish and support high academic standards, and operate at a cost comparable to today's schools."

The organization began by selecting design teams to plan new models of schooling. The NASDC models are being field tested in schools in many communities throughout the United States. NASDC believes in using diverse design strategies to benefit the communities to be served (from rural Mississippi to inner-city Los Angeles to a Native American reservation in Minnesota), but all of the schools are unified by seven principles:

70

- High academic STANDARDS.
- Strong ACCOUNTABILITY and ASSESSMENT measures.
- Thematic, interactive, project-based CURRICULUM and strategies.
- Ongoing PROFESSIONAL DEVELOPMENT.
- Parent and community involvement.
- Flexible school governance.
- Integration of technology.

Resources: A Guide to New American Schools. Available from Education Commission of the States, Suite 2700, 707 17th St., Denver, CO 80202-3427, tel. 303/299-3692.

New American Schools Development Corp., Suite 2710, 1000 Wilson Blvd., Arlington, VA 22209, tel. 703/908-9500.

New Standards

A partnership project that involves the National Center on Education and the Economy, the Learning Research and Development Center at the University of Pittsburgh, and states and large school districts. The project's goal is to set high U.S. academic standards and to measure the progress of the students by using a performance assessment system that includes PORTFOLIOS, EXHIBITIONS and performances, and projects, both in groups and alone, all based on real-life tasks.

Several thousand schools in about 20 states are involved in this project. New Standards is committed to bringing world-class standards to minority and low-income children.

The project worked on building PERFORMANCE TASKS and assessments from 1991 to 1993, then began piloting a PORTFOLIO ASSESSMENT system with 50,000 students in 4th, 8th, and 10th grades. Project directors are BENCHMARKING work of international students and school systems while researching public opinion concerning appropriate levels of performance for U.S. students.

Resources: Learning Research and Development Center, New Standards, Room 310, 3939 O'Hara St., University of Pittsburgh, Pittsburgh, PA 15260, tel. 412/624-8319.

National Center on Education and the Economy, New Standards Project, Suite 750, 700 11th St. NW, Washington, DC 20001, tel. 202/783-3668.

71

nongraded or ungraded school A way of organizing schools that uses individual student progress to determine when students move from one level of schooling to another. In an ungraded primary school, some students take longer than others to move into 4th grade from a primary-level multi-age classroom (kindergarten through 3rd grade). Students are not classified by grade levels and not evaluated using traditional letter grades (A,B,C,D,F) but their achievement is carefully monitored. As part of a major school reform in Kentucky, all schools in that state are expected to have a nongraded primary school. The idea is that children ages 5–8 can progress at their own pace without fear of failure, and that they learn best through well-planned activities appropriate to each child's level of development.

Resources: How to Change to a Nongraded School, by M. Hunter. Available from ASCD, 1250 N. Pitt St., Alexandria, VA 22314-1453, tel. 703/549-9110, or 800/933-2723. Internet: http://www.ascd.org

Nongradedness: Helping It to Happen, by R. Anderson and B. Pavan. Lancaster, Pa.: Technomic Pub. Co.

"Without Fear of Failure: The Attributes of an Ungraded Primary School," by N.B. Privett. *The School Administrator,* January 1996, pp. 6–11.

norm-referenced tests   Standardized tests designed to measure how a student's performance compares with the scores of other students who took the test for norming purposes. Most standardized achievement tests are NORM-REFERENCED, meaning that a student's performance is compared to the performances of students in a norming group. Scores on norm-referenced tests are often reported in terms of grade-level equivalencies or percentiles derived from the scores of the original students. See CRITERION-REFERENCED tests.

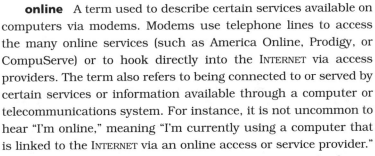

online   A term used to describe certain services available on computers via modems. Modems use telephone lines to access the many online services (such as America Online, Prodigy, or CompuServe) or to hook directly into the INTERNET via access providers. The term also refers to being connected to or served by certain services or information available through a computer or telecommunications system. For instance, it is not uncommon to hear "I'm online," meaning "I'm currently using a computer that is linked to the INTERNET via an online access or service provider."

Online services include data banks of research and information, current news, travel information, games, live chat sessions (in chat rooms, in which users type conversations on a topic or similar interests), and electronic mail (a service through which users write and send messages via a modem).

Resources: Computer Life, Family PC, and *Home PC* articles are written to give laypeople information about the latest computer products and trends.

opportunity-to-learn standards   Ensuring that all students have the resources and conditions they need to reach the same high performance STANDARDS. Advocates of opportunity-to-learn standards, also known as school delivery standards, believe that if government is to specify minimum standards for what students should know and be able to do, they should also specify what schools must provide students, including CURRICULUM, instruction, and classroom equipment. For example, some students might be able to meet performance standards only if they have ESL or BILINGUAL classes or SPECIAL-NEEDS resources.

outcomes   Intended results of schooling: What students are supposed to know and be able to do. William G. Spady, an advocate of outcome-based education, recommends that schools state outcomes in terms of what they expect students to demonstrate at the end of an instructional experience. Educators and others may use the term outcomes to mean roughly the same as GOALS, objectives, or even STANDARDS.

Resources: "Choosing Outcomes of Significance," by William G. Spady. *Educational Leadership*, March 1994, pp. 18–23.

Outcome-Based Education: Critical Issues and Answers, by W.G. Spady. Available from American Association of School Administrators, 1801 N. Moore St., Arlington, VA 22209, tel. 703/528-0700.

74

outcome-based education   An approach to schooling that makes outcomes—intended results—the key factor in planning and creating educational experiences. Adherents of outcome-based education (OBE) say that, ideally, the amount of time spent learning, and other factors, such as what the student does to learn, should depend on the outcome to be achieved. In conventional schooling, they say, time is fixed and outcomes are variable. OBE advocates believe outcomes should be fixed and time should be variable.

The OBE movement grew from a concern that students were graduating from high school without having mastered the basic knowledge and skills needed to participate in adult society. Adherents proposed that students should be expected to demonstrate what they had learned and that high school graduation should be based on such demonstrated learning.

William G. Spady, a leader in the OBE movement for 20 years, explains that outcome-based education is "inherently about defining, raising, and accomplishing clearer, higher standards of learning and performance for more students," and that it does this by providing a precise focus, emphasizing what is learned rather than how it is learned, designing teaching and learning based on the desired outcomes, and increasing students' opportunities to succeed (*Education Week,* March 6, 1996).

OBE has many opponents, including traditionalist organizations who object to educators' tendencies to state values as outcomes and their declared intent to equalize outcomes by downplaying competition. Opponents insist that trying to get all students to meet the same high standards is "dumbing down" education, because standards will be lower for those who are now most successful.

Resources: *Educational Leadership,* March 1994. Theme issue on "The Challenge of Outcome-Based Education." Available from ASCD, 1250 N. Pitt St., Alexandria, VA 22314-1453, tel. 703/549-9110, or 800/933-2723. Internet: http://www.ascd.org

Outcome-Based Education. Video series. Available from ASCD, 1250 N. Pitt St., Alexandria, VA 22314-1453, tel. 703/549-9110, or 800/933-2723. Internet: http://www.ascd.org

Outcome-Based Education: Critical Issues and Answers, by William G. Spady. Available from American Association of School Administrators, 1801 N. Moore St., Arlington, VA 22209, tel. 703/528-0700.

Understanding the Conflict over Outcome-Based Education. Two 90-minute audiocassettes. Available from ASCD, 1250 N. Pitt St., Alexandria, VA 22314-1453, tel. 703/549-9110, or 800/933-2723. Internet: http://www.ascd.org

Paideia An approach to school reform proposed by philosopher Mortimer Adler in 1982 in *The Paideia Proposal: An Education Manifesto* (New York: MacMillan). Unlike many reform ideas that try to individualize the CURRICULUM to fit each student's needs and strengths, Paideia calls for all students to study a single-track, rigorous curriculum. The only elective is foreign language. Paideia's curriculum calls for three methods of learning: didactic teaching (lecture), the Socratic method (in which a teacher uses directed questioning to help students arrive at desirable answers), and COACHING.

Resource: "Launching Paideia in Chattanooga," by C.M. Gettys and A. Wheelock. *Educational Leadership,* September 1994, pp. 12–15.

parent involvement Studies show that students do better in school when their parents or guardians are involved and encouraging. Options for involvement include a wide array of commitments of time and talent, from reading a story to a class once a week to a one-time presentation about a person's career for a group of high school juniors.

Parents who cannot volunteer need to be aware that parent involvement is far more than school volunteering. It also encompasses attending evening events at their children's schools, raising funds for school clubs and sports, or attending a PTA or school board meeting. Perhaps the most important type of parent involvement happens at home: reading notes that come home from school, looking over children's homework with them, talking about the school day, and reading together make a difference in a child's attitude and progress in school. See FAMILY INVOLVEMENT INITIATIVE.

Resources: Education Today is a newsletter written to keep busy parents informed about education issues, from new policies and reform ideas to making the most of routine school events, such as parent-teacher conferences. Educational Publishing Group, 20 Park Plaza, Ste. 1215, Boston, MA 02116, tel. 800/927-6006, ext. 127.

The *Education Today Parent Involvement Handbook.* Educational Publishing Group, 20 Park Plaza, Ste. 1215, Boston, MA 02116, tel. 800/927-6006, ext. 127.

The Family Education Network at http://www.familyeducation.com is a full-service Web offering on helping children succeed in school and beyond.

How to Involve Parents in a Multicultural School, by B. Davis. Available from ASCD, 1250 N. Pitt St., Alexandria, VA 22314-1453, tel. 703/549-9110, or 800/933-2723. Internet: http://www.ascd.org

The National Association of Elementary School Principals (NAESP) has several brochures and videos on parent involvement. NAESP, 1615 Duke St., Alexandria, VA 22314, tel. 703/684-3345, or 800/386-2377.

77

partnerships   A word frequently added to discussions of school reform, partnerships refer to one or more combinations of community and school alliances that can enrich and strengthen the schools. Examples of partnerships include school and community partnerships, family and school partnerships, and BUSINESS AND SCHOOL PARTNERSHIPS.

pedagogy   The art of teaching, especially conscious use of particular instructional methods. If a teacher uses a discovery approach rather than direct instruction, for example, she is using a different pedagogy.

peer mediation   See CONFLICT RESOLUTION.

performance tasks   Activities, exercises, or problems that require students to show what they can do. Some performance tasks are designed to have students demonstrate their understanding by applying their knowledge to a particular situation. For example, students might be given a current political map of Africa showing the names and locations of countries and a similar map from 1945 and be asked to identify and explain differences and similarities. To be more authentic (more like what someone might be expected to do in the adult world), the task might be to prepare a newspaper article explaining the changes.

Performance tasks often have more than one acceptable solution; they may call for a student to create a response to a problem and then explain or defend it. The process involves the use of HIGHER-ORDER THINKING SKILLS (e.g., cause and effect analysis, deductive or inductive reasoning, experimentation, and problem solving). Performance tasks may be used primarily for assessment at the end of a period of instruction, but are frequently used for learning as well as assessment.

78

Resources: *Assessing Student Outcomes: Performance Assessment Using the Dimensions of Learning Model,* by R. Marzano, D. Pickering, and J. McTighe. Available from ASCD, 1250 N. Pitt St., Alexandria, VA 22314-1453, tel. 703/549-9110, or 800/933-2723. Internet: http://www.ascd.org

A Teacher's Guide to Performance-Based Learning and Assessment, by educators in Connecticut's Pomperaug School District 15. ASCD, 1250 N. Pitt St., Alexandria, VA 22314-1453, tel. 703/549-9110, or 800/933-2723. Internet: http://www.ascd.org

personalization   Schooling that emphasizes the needs of students as individual persons. To personalize learning, teachers must be able to adapt to students' individual interests and styles, so they must know students well. The term is sometimes used to contrast personalization with INDIVIDUALIZED INSTRUCTION, which may be considered more technical and procedural. Schoolwide provisions for personalization may include smaller classes, ADVISORY SYSTEMS, independent study, and student-parent-teacher conferences.

phonics   The relationship between the basic sounds (phonemes) of a language and the way those sounds are represented by symbols (letters of the alphabet). Many people see phonics as a method of teaching reading that begins with the study of individual letter sounds (44 basic sounds in English), progressing to words that contain those sounds, and then to reading the words in stories. From this standpoint, phonics is opposite in theory and technique from the WHOLE LANGUAGE approach to reading. However, many teachers say they are teaching phonics when they teach sound-letter correspondence as part of an INTEGRATED LANGUAGE ARTS program.

Marie Carbo, an expert on reading styles, contends that one method of teaching reading is not inherently better than the other. Different methods work for different students because of their individual abilities and LEARNING STYLES. Problems arise when a teacher or organization promotes one theory to the exclusion of another without considering the needs and strengths of individual students.

Resource: "Reading Styles: High Gains for the Bottom Third," by M. Carbo. *Educational Leadership*, February 1996, pp. 8–13.

portfolio   A collection of student work chosen to exemplify and document a student's learning progress. Just as professional artists assemble portfolios of their work, students are often encouraged or required to maintain a portfolio illustrating various aspects of their learning. Some teachers specify what student work is to be included, while others let students decide. Portfolios are a valuable way to assess student learning because they include multiple examples of student work and are specifically intended to document growth over time. They are difficult to score reliably and may be a logistical problem for teachers, but educators say that portfolios help stimulate student reflection. Portfolios are primarily a tool for teaching and learning, but some educational agencies are experimenting with also using them for ACCOUNTABILITY.

79

Resources: Assessment for Standards, IBM Research, 30 Saw Mill Road, Hawthorne, NY 10532, tel. 914/784-6603.

Digital Portfolios, Coalition of Essential Schools, c/o Brown University, P.O. Box 1969, Providence, RI 02912, tel. 401/863-3384.

The Mindful School: The Portfolio Connection, by K. Burke, R. Fogarty, and S. Belgrad. Available from ERIC, Clearinghouse on Assessment and Evaluation, The Catholic University of America, 210 O'Boyle Hall, Washington, DC 20064, tel. 202/319-5120, or 800/ 464-37642. Fax 202/319-6692. E-mail: eric_ae@cua.edu.

Student Portfolios, NEA Teacher to Teacher Books. Available from the

National Education Association Professional Library, 1201 16th Street, N.W., Washington, D.C. 20036, tel. 800/229-4200, or 202/822-7207.

privatized schools   Public schools run by a for-profit company. The company usually assumes control of one or more existing public schools that the local board or some other government agency has decided to turn over to a private company for management.

The two largest corporations involved in privatization are the EDISON PROJECT and Educational Alternatives Inc. (EAI). Both organizations claim that they can run schools more successfully on smaller budgets than those managed by public school districts. The movement toward privatization began in 1988 when a school system in Chelsea, Mass., chose to be managed privately by Boston University.

Advocates of privatization believe that failing schools can benefit from more efficient management and from competition. Opponents dislike the idea that these corporations make money by educating children and argue that the funds should instead be used for teachers, equipment, and supplies. Some people believe that children with SPECIAL NEEDS will be ignored in the competition to save money.

Resource: Educational Leadership, September 1994. Theme issue on "The New Alternative Schools."

problem-based learning   An approach to curriculum and teaching that involves students in solution of real-life problems rather than conventional study of terms and information. Developed in leading medical schools, problem-based learning begins with a real problem that connects to the student's world, such as how to upgrade a local waste treatment plant. Student teams organize their methods and procedures around specifics of the problem, not around subject matter as such. Students explore various avenues before arriving at a solution to present to the class.

Teachers report that students using problem-based learning, which is similar to AUTHENTIC LEARNING and INTERDISCIPLINARY LEARNING, become more interested in their studies, more motivated to explore in-depth, and more likely to see the value of the lesson.

Problems are chosen for their appropriateness and power to illuminate core concepts in the school's curriculum. They must be carefully selected to ensure that students learn the necessary content.

Resource: "Problem-Based Learning: As Authentic As It Gets," by W. Stepien and Shelagh Gallagher. *Educational Leadership*, April 1993, pp. 25–28.

professional development   Also known as staff development, this term refers to experiences, such as attending conferences and workshops, that help teachers and administrators build knowledge and skills.

Project Zero   An education research project founded at the Harvard Graduate School of Education in 1967 by philosopher Nelson Goodman. Goodman believed that "arts learning should be studied as a serious cognitive activity, but that close to 'zero' had been established in the field." Today Project Zero is concerned not only with the arts, but also with education across all disciplines and in various settings.

The Project Zero programs are based on understanding how individuals develop. At the heart of the educational process is the student, who must be respected for unique learning development, perceptions, and styles. Howard Gardner (see also MULTIPLE INTELLIGENCES) is a director of Project Zero's Development Group.

One of the many undertakings of Project Zero is ATLAS: Communities for Authentic Teaching, Learning, and Assessment for All Students, which is working with the COALITION OF ESSENTIAL SCHOOLS at Brown University, the School Development Program at Yale University, and the Education Development Center in Newton, Mass. The goal is to design school CURRICULA around ESSENTIAL QUESTIONS, such as "What is freedom?" ATLAS is one of the design teams for the NEW AMERICAN SCHOOLS DEVELOPMENT CORPORATION.

Resources: *Art, Mind, and Brain: A Cognitive Approach to Creativity*, by H. Gardner. Available from Basic Books, 10 E. 53 St., New York, NY 10022, tel. 800/638-3030.

Project Zero, Third Floor, Longfellow Hall, Harvard Graduate School of Education, Cambridge, MA 02138, tel. 617/495-4342.

81

qualitative research   Research that uses methods adapted from anthropology and other social sciences, including systematic observation and interviews. Until recently, most educational research was QUANTITATIVE. Some researchers are now using qualitative methods because they think statistical processes will not produce the understandings they seek. For example, a researcher might spend an entire year visiting a particular school, observing classes, meetings, and conversations, seeking to identify the way decisions are made and the roles played by various staff members.

quantitative research   Research conducted in a traditional scientific manner using statistical procedures to compare the effects of one treatment with another. For example, a researcher might compare test scores of students taught using an experimental method with the scores of students taught in a "traditional" way. Some researchers now see this approach as limited, so make greater use of QUALITATIVE RESEARCH methods.

ready to learn   A phrase that refers to preparing children for school with the attitudes, knowledge, and skills needed to succeed. When referring to students who will soon begin kindergarten or 1st grade, getting students ready to learn means enriching their preschool environment so that they know some basics, including the alphabet, how to count to 10, and the names of shapes and colors. The phrase also refers to ensuring that all students have basic necessities, including enough sleep, good nutrition, and a safe environment at home and at school. See also SCHOOL READINESS.

remedial education   Remedial education, so-called because it remedies a situation, is supposed to enable students to catch up with their peers. For example, reading classes at the high school or college level are considered remedial because most students learn to read in elementary school. However, researchers observe that remedial classes sometimes teach low-level skills and convey low expectations.

Resource: Up from Underachievement: How Teachers, Students, and Parents Can Work Together to Promote Student Success, by D. Heacox. Available from Free Spirit Press, Suite 616, 400 First Ave. North, Minneapolis, MN 55401, tel. 612/338-2068, or 800/735-7323.

resource room   Occasionally still called the special education room, the resource room is a specified place in a school building where students can go for additional help mastering specific skills, and where alternative methods of teaching and small-group or one-on-one instruction are offered. Some schools offer this resource to any student who desires help in a given subject area, but usually students with LEARNING DISABILITIES or other SPECIAL NEEDS are assigned to the resource room for a certain number of hours each week.

restructuring   The implementation of new organizational patterns and styles of leadership and management to bring about renewed, more effective schools. Reforms may include changing the roles of teachers and administrators, allocating more decision-making power to teachers, involving parents in decisions, or reorganizing the school day or year.

84

Restructuring is, among other things, a change from top-down decision making to COLLABORATIVE decision making, and it recognizes teachers' professionalism and knowledge of their students and curriculum. The purpose of school restructuring is to set clear goals and create a learning environment that is conducive to reaching those goals.

See also SYSTEMIC REFORM, SCHOOL RESTRUCTURING, and SCHOOL-BASED MANAGEMENT.

Resources: *Assisting Change in Education,* by E. Saxl, M. Miles, and A. Lieberman. Available from ASCD, 1250 N. Pitt St., Alexandria, VA 22314-1453, tel. 703/549-9110, or 800/933-2723. Internet: http://www.ascd.org

Readings from Educational Leadership: Restructuring Schools, Available from ASCD, 1250 N. Pitt St., Alexandria, VA 22314-1453, tel. 703/549-9110, or 800/933-2723. Internet: http://www.ascd.org

Restructuring Schooling: Learning from Ongoing Efforts, edited by J. Murphy and P. Hallinger. Newbury Park, Ca.: Corwin Press.

Schools for the 21st Century, by P.C. Schlechty. Available from Jossey-Bass Publishers, 350 Sansome St., San Francisco, CA 94104, tel. 415/433-1740, or 800/956-7739. Internet: http://www.josseybass.com

The Self-Renewing School, by B. Joyce, J. Wolf, and E. Calhoun. Available from ASCD, 1250 N. Pitt St., Alexandria, VA 22314-1453, tel. 703/549-9110, 800/933-2723. Internet: http://www.ascd.org

rubric   Specific descriptions of what a particular performance looks like at several different levels of quality. Rubrics are
used to evaluate student performance on PERFORMANCE TASKS that
cannot be scored by machine. Students are given or help develop
a rubric (often with three or four levels) that describes what they
might accomplish through a given performance.

For example, the content of an oral presentation might be
evaluated using the following rubric:

Level 4   The main idea is well developed, using important
details and anecdotes. The information is accurate
and impressive. The topic is thoroughly developed
within time constraints.

Level 3   The main idea is reasonably clear and supporting
details are adequate and relevant. The information
is accurate. The topic is adequately developed within time constraints, but is not complete.

Level 2   The main idea is not clearly indicated. Some information is inaccurate. The topic is supported with
few details and is sketchy and incomplete.

Level 1   A main idea is not evident. The information has
many inaccuracies. The topic is not supported with
details.

85

86

Safe Schools Act   Part of the GOALS 2000: EDUCATE AMERICA ACT legislation, the Safe Schools Act provides funding to local education agencies for violence prevention programs, including peer mediation, counseling, and teacher training. In addition, the Gun-Free Schools Act requires that any student who brings a gun to school must be expelled for at least one year. Certain exceptions apply.

The Safe and Drug-Free Schools and Communities Act provides funding to communities and states for violence and drug prevention programs.

Resources: Department of Education at 800/USA-LEARN.

Safe At School: Awareness and Action for Parents of Kids Grades K–12, by C.S. Saunders. Available from Free Spirit Press, Suite 616, 400 First Avenue North, Minneapolis, MN 55401, tel. 612/338-2068, or 800/735-7323.

scaffolding   The way a teacher provides support to make sure students succeed at complex tasks they couldn't do otherwise. Most teaching is done as the students go about the task, rather than before they start.

For example, as a group of elementary students proceed to publish a student newspaper, the teacher shows them how to conduct interviews, write news stories, and prepare captions for photographs. Because the teacher supports the students to make sure they don't fail in their effort, it reminds researchers of the scaffolding that workers sometimes place around buildings. As the students become more skillful, the teacher gives them more responsibility, taking away the scaffolding when it is no longer needed. (This gradual withdrawal has been called "fading.")

SCANS (Secretary's Commission on Achieving Necessary Skills) Report A report issued by the U.S. Department of Labor that attempts to identify the knowledge, skills, and abilities that workers need to succeed in entry-level jobs. SCANS highlights necessary competencies in basic skills (reading, writing, math, listening, and speaking), thinking skills (creative thinking, decision making, problem solving, visualizing symbols, reasoning, and knowing how to learn), and personal qualities (responsibility, self-esteem, sociability, self-management, and integrity). The goal is to use these requirements to develop educational curricula.

87

See also SCHOOL-TO-WORK.

Resources: College and the Workplace: How Should We Assess Student Performance? by Peter Cappelli. Available from National Center on Educational Quality of the Workforce, #WP09, University of Pennsylvania, 4200 Pine St., 5A, Philadelphia, PA 19104, tel. 800/437-9799.

Learning A Living: A Blueprint for High Performance—Part I. Available from Government Printing Office. Call 212/512-1800 or fax 212/512-2250. Stock no. 029-000-00439-1. http://www.jhu.edu/~LPs/scans/principles.html describes SCANS principles and recommendations.

What Work Requires of Schools: A SCANS Report for America 2000, (Washington, D.C.: U.S. Dept. of Labor, 1991). Single copies available from National Technical Information Service (NTIS), Operations Division, Springfield, VA 22151. NTIS no. PB92-146711.

Scholastic Achievement Tests (SAT II; formerly ACH) Administered by The College Board, these are subject-matter tests. Many colleges require that students applying for admission take the English exam and one other subject exam.

An essay has been added to the English exam. In 1994, the College Board added Japanese and Chinese language exams and audio portions to all of the foreign-language exams.

Resource: The College Board, 45 Columbus Ave., New York, NY 10023-6992, tel. 717/348-9287, or 212/713-8165.

Scholastic Assessment Test (SAT I) Formerly called the Scholastic Aptitude Test, the SAT was introduced in the 1950s and renamed in 1994. The SAT is one of two standardized tests used by colleges as a primary basis for evaluating a student's application for admission. According to The College Board, the name now reflects more accurately what the exam does: It measures what a student has learned, not what a student might hope to accomplish in life.

Changes in the SAT include 10 fill-in-the-blank math questions, longer reading passages with more weight in the scoring process, more vocabulary words used in context, and allowing the use of a calculator.

Beginning April 1, 1995, the College Board recentered the median score of the SAT to 500. Many critics believe that this adjustment amounts to padding and attempts to hide declining SAT scores. The College Board says that the alteration better reflects the mid-range score. The SAT I is taken each year by 1.2 million students from a variety of cultures, economic conditions, regions, and schools.

Resources: The College Board, 45 Columbus Ave., New York, NY 10023-6992, tel. 717/348-9287, or 212/713-8165.

Standing Up to the SAT, by J. Weiss, B. Beckworth, and B. Schaeffer. Available from the University of Chicago Press, 11030 South Langley Ave., Chicago, IL 60628, tel. 800/621-2736.

school-based management A bottom-up approach to school governance that gives increased decision-making authority to staff members at the school. School- or site-based management teams are usually composed of administrators, teachers, and parents; some include student representatives, community members, and one or more business partners. Team members share responsibility for educational, leadership, and administrative functions. School-based management often emphasizes decision making by consensus in areas that may include setting goals, choosing textbooks, hiring teachers and administrators, and allocating funds to school projects.

Resources: ASCD Pocket Guides to School-Based Management, by A. Dornseif. (1996). A series of eight pocket guides, each focusing on an important SBM topic. Contact ASCD for specific titles, 1250 N. Pitt St.,

Alexandria, VA 22314-1453, tel. 703/549-9110, or 800/933-2723. Internet: http://www.ascd.org

"Making School-Based Management Work," by E.R. Odden and P. Wohlstetter. *Educational Leadership*, February 1995, pp. 32–36.

school choice The idea that families should have more than one alternative when enrolling their children in school. Some school districts and states provide options in public schools in the form of CHARTER or MAGNET SCHOOLS. School choice has also come to mean choice beyond public schools, by way of school VOUCHERS to be used at private schools.

Advocates of school choice argue that it encourages healthy competition among schools for enrollment, thus raising the quality of all schools. Opponents fear that preferred schools will receive more funding, thus causing a greater equity gap.

Resource: *Essential Questions on Public School Choice.* Available from Education Commission of the States, Suite 2700, 707 17th St., Denver, CO 80202-3427, tel. 303/299-3692.

89

school climate and **school culture** The sum of the values, cultures, safety practices, and organizational structures within a school that cause it to function and react in particular ways. Some schools are said to have a nurturing environment that recognizes children and treats them as individuals; others may have the feel of authoritarian structures where rules are strictly enforced and hierarchical control is strong. Teaching practices, diversity, and the relationships among administrators, teachers, parents, and students contribute to school climate. Although the two terms are somewhat interchangeable, school climate refers mostly to the school's effects on students, while school culture refers more to the way teachers and other staff members work together.

school-linked programs See COMMUNITY CENTER SCHOOLS.

school readiness The basic background and knowledge that children "ought" to have upon entering kindergarten. Some educators believe that school readiness skills should include:

• Recognition of colors and basic shapes.

• Gross motor coordination that enables children to catch a ball.
• Fine motor coordination that enables them to hold a crayon or pencil.
• The ability to sort objects (e.g., beans or coins).
• Knowing their first and last names and home address.

In addition, school readiness is usually thought to include, for example, good nutrition, medical shots and care, safety, and guidance. Some programs, including HEAD START, attempt to boost the preschool development of children from low socioeconomic backgrounds.

Resources: *Ready or Not: What Parents Should Know About School Readiness.* Available from National Association for the Education of Young Children, 1509 16th St. NW, Washington, DC 20036, tel. 202/232-8777, or 800/424-2460.

Starting Points: Meeting the Needs of Our Youngest Children, by Carnegie Corporation of New York. Available from Carnegie Corporation of New York, 437 Madison Ave., New York, NY 10022, tel. 212/371-3200. Internet: http://www.carnegie.org

Starting School: A Parent's Guide to the Kindergarten Year. Available from Modern Learning Press/Programs for Education, P.O. Box 167, Rosemont, NJ 08556, tel. 609/397-2214, or 800/627-5867.

school restructuring   See RESTRUCTURING

school-to-work   A movement based on the belief that students are not adequately prepared for careers by the time they graduate from high school. Although a growing number of parents believe their children must attend college and earn at least a bachelor's degree to make a comfortable living, nearly three-quarters of U.S. citizens do not have a college degree, indicating that high school graduates need preparation and training to succeed in the work world.

The School-to-Work Opportunities Act broadens educational, career, and economic opportunities for all students by creating partnerships between schools and businesses, community organizations, and government agencies. The act funds a variety of programs, including apprenticeships, TECH PREP programs, and internships. Schools and businesses work together to integrate learning and job-training skills. Goals of the School-to-Work Opportunities Act:

90

- Students receive both a meaningful high school diploma and a skill certificate recognized by employers.
- Employers have more access to a trained and skilled workforce.
- The United States will have a competent and highly educated workforce capable of prospering in a global economy.

Resources: Center on Education and Work, University of Wisconsin-Madison, 964 Educational Sciences Building, 1025 W. Johnson St., Madison, WI 53706, tel. 608/263-2929.

Jobs for the Future, One Bowdoin Square, Boston, MA 02140, tel. 617/742-5995.

National Occupational Information Coordinating Committee, Suite 156, 2100 M St. NW, Washington, DC 20037, tel. 202/653-5665.

School-to-Work Resources. Internet: http://www.nhmccd.cc.tx.us/groups.stw/resource.html.

self-renewing schools   Schools that have developed the capacity to revise their structures and processes to adapt to changing conditions. Self-renewing schools are sometimes called learning organizations because they learn and change in response to experiences. Advocates of self-renewing schools believe that schools should change traditional practices that do not fit modern conditions, such as programs developed for parents at a time when most mothers were not employed outside their home.

Resources: Educational Leadership, April 1995. Theme issue on "Self-Renewing Schools."

The Self-Renewing School, by B. Joyce, J. Wolf, E. Calhoun. ASCD, 1250 N. Pitt St., Alexandria, VA 22314-1453, tel. 703/549-9110, or 800/933-2723. Internet: http://www.ascd.org

service learning   An educational practice designed to enrich students' learning, connect their learning to life experiences, and increase their self-esteem through community service work. Some schools, businesses, and social organizations offer opportunities for students to work in soup kitchens, recycling centers, homeless shelters, and community hospital fairs.

Some schools require that students earn a certain number of credits in service learning in order to graduate.

91

Resources: Enriching the Curriculum Through Service Learning, edited by C.W. Kinsley and K. McPherson. Available from ASCD, 1250 N. Pitt St., Alexandria, VA 22314-1453, tel. 703/549-9110, or 800/933-2723. Internet: http://www.ascd.org

How to Establish a High School Service Learning Program, by J. Witmer and C.S. Anderson. Available from ASCD, 1250 N. Pitt St., Alexandria, VA 22314-1453, tel. 703/549-9110, or 800/933-2723. Internet: http://www.ascd.org

The Kid's Guide to Service Projects, by B.A. Lewis. Available from Free Spirit Press, Suite 616, 400 First Avenue North, Minneapolis, MN 55401, tel. 612/338-2068, or 800/735-7323.

Standards of Quality for School-Based and Community-Based Service Learning. Available from the Alliance for Service Learning in Education Reform, Close Up Foundation, 44 Canal Center Plaza, Alexandria, VA 22314.

site-based management   See SCHOOL-BASED MANAGEMENT.

social promotion   The practice of promoting students to the next grade whether or not they have accomplished the goals of their current grade. Opponents argue that social promotion can produce functionally illiterate graduates, whereas supporters point to research indicating that retained students are much more likely to drop out of school and engage in AT-RISK behaviors.

special education   Generally refers to teaching students who require additional instructional aids, access to a RESOURCE ROOM, specially trained teachers, innovative technology, and external placement to reach their potential. Students may be recommended for special education because of LEARNING DISABILITIES, developmental disorders, physical impairments, or other SPECIAL NEEDS. The term occasionally includes those considered GIFTED.

Resource: Critical Issues in Special Education, by B. Algozzine, M. Thurlow, and J. Ysseldyke. Boston: Houghton Mifflin.

special-needs students   Those students who, because of physical, developmental, behavioral, or emotional difficulties, require SPECIAL EDUCATION to succeed. Students with LEARNING DISABILITIES (LD) are special-needs students, but not all special-needs students have learning disabilities as defined by law. For example, children diagnosed with ATTENTION DEFICIT (HYPERACTIVITY)

DISORDER need additional services and particular learning environments to succeed, but federal law does not provide for them as it does for children with DYSLEXIA or autism. Other special-needs students not covered by the INDIVIDUALS WITH DISABILITIES EDUCATION ACT include those with emotional disturbances.

Sometimes the category of special-needs students includes GIFTED AND TALENTED students.

standardized testing   See ASSESSMENT.

standards   Statements of what students should know and be able to do. Different types of standards address various aspects important to learning:

- Content standards cover what students are to learn in various subject areas, such as mathematics and science.
- Performance standards specify what levels of learning are expected.
- OPPORTUNITY-TO-LEARN standards state the conditions and resources necessary to give all students an equal chance to meet performance standards.
- WORLD-CLASS STANDARDS indicate content and performances that are expected of students in other industrialized countries. This term is also attached to the movement in the United States to bring U.S. students' academic achievement and knowledge on par with students' accomplishments in the other industrialized countries.

Resources: How to Use Standards in the Classroom, by D. Harris, J. Carr, T. Flynn, M. Petit, and S. Rigney. (1996). Available from ASCD, 1250 N. Pitt St., Alexandria, VA 22314-1453, tel. (703) 549-9110, or (800) 933-2723. Internet: http://www.ascd.org

Standards-Driven Education. Available from Education Commission of the States, Suite 2700, 707 17th St., Denver, CO 80202-3427, tel. 303/299-3692.

student-led conference   A variation of the traditional parent-teacher conference. The students prepare for the conference and lead it by showing their parents or family members samples of their schoolwork, often in the form of portfolios, and discussing areas of strengths and weaknesses.

Proponents feel that student achievement increases as the student takes more responsibility for preparing and demonstrat-

93

ing work. In addition, it gives students an opportunity to practice presentation skills. If parents need a private talk with the teacher, a separate meeting or phone conversation is usually arranged.

Student Loan Reform Act See INDIVIDUAL EDUCATION ACCOUNTS.

summative test A test given to evaluate and document what students have learned. The term is used to distinguish such tests from FORMATIVE tests, which are used primarily to diagnose what students have learned in order to plan further instruction.

supervision The process by which one person, usually someone with greater authority, helps another person improve his or her performance. A persistent issue in education is the relationship between supervision and teacher evaluation. In education, supervision is ideally a nonthreatening and helping relationship, and teacher evaluation is a formal administrative responsibility. In practice, most supervision is done by the school principal by visiting the teacher's classroom to observe and then meeting with the teacher to discuss the effectiveness of the lesson. The process of observing and conferring is sometimes called clinical supervision to distinguish it from the kind of employee supervision necessary in any organization, such as making sure people get to work on time.

Resource: *Supervision in Transition,* 1992 ASCD Yearbook, edited by C. D. Glickman. Available from ASCD, 1250 N. Pitt St., Alexandria, VA 22314-1453, tel. 703/549-9110, or 800/933-2723. Internet: http://www.ascd.org

systemic reform Improvement of education by coordinating all aspects of the system—which may be a state, a local district, or even a school. Recognizing that regulations and tradition sometimes interfere with reform, policy makers talk about STANDARDS-based systemic reform, meaning establishment of performance standards students are to meet (usually at the state level), and then aligning everything else—CURRICULUM, ASSESSMENT, college entrance requirements, teacher education, teacher certification, teacher PROFESSIONAL DEVELOPMENT, and so on—with the

94

expected standards. If goals call for students to learn content they are not learning now, new instructional materials may be needed, new tests may have to be created, and teachers may need to learn new approaches. All parts of the system must work together.

Resource: *Systemic Education Reform,* by J. Thompson. Available from ERIC Clearinghouse on Educational Management, 5207 University of Oregon, 1787 Agate St., Eugene, OR 97403-5207, tel. 503/346-2334, or 800/438-8841.

teacher certification Official recognition, ordinarily by the state, that a person is qualified to be a teacher. A single certification used to last a lifetime, but many states now require certificate renewal every few years, with evidence of the completion of university or district inservice courses. Many teaching certificates are highly specialized by subject, grade levels, or specifics such as counseling or the ability to teach students with disabilities.

ALTERNATIVE CERTIFICATION is a way for persons without the standard qualifications to teach while learning on the job (with continuing education and supervision).

teacher portfolios Collections of items or exhibits intended to show a teacher's accomplishments and abilities. The idea comes from student PORTFOLIOS, which may supplement or replace tests of student learning. Similarly, teacher portfolios can be used as a means of evaluation. The teacher certification program being pioneered by the NATIONAL BOARD FOR PROFESSIONAL TEACHING STANDARDS uses teacher portfolios.

team teaching A strategy that allows two or more teachers to work together with a group of students. The teachers may work together to teach the same group all of the coursework for that year, or they may team together to create a specific unit of study. The latter strategy is frequently used in creating an INTERDISCIPLINARY unit of study.

Resource: Teams in Education: Creating an Integrated Approach, by J.S. Arcaro. Available from St. Lucie Press, Suite 403B, 100 E. Linton Blvd., Delray Beach, FL 33483, tel. 407/274-9906.

tech prep   Programs of study that help prepare students for careers by teaching them computer and technology skills. Most tech-prep courses include two years of training in high school and two years in a community college. Although this educational alternative is intended to prepare students for good jobs without a college degree, many students who enter these programs continue their education in a four-year college or university. See also SCHOOL-TO-WORK and VOCATIONAL EDUCATION.

Resource: Tech Prep: Effective & Promising Practices Guide. Available from the Center on Education and Work, Publications, 964 Educational Sciences Building, 1025 West Johnson St., Madison, WI 53706, tel. 608/263-2929, or 800/446-0399.

97

Title I (formerly Chapter 1)   Part of the IMPROVING AMERICA'S SCHOOLS ACT OF 1994, Title I primarily benefits poor and disadvantaged children in more than 50,000 schools in the United States. About five million of the children in these schools live in high-poverty areas. Title I programs, first established in 1965, focus on improved teaching and learning to help AT-RISK students achieve higher standards, and include extended day-care programs, transitions from preschool to elementary school, and greater parent involvement.

Title I includes an emphasis on higher learning standards and state assessments for measuring student progress.

tracking   The practice of grouping students according to their perceived abilities. While this practice is most noticeable or more commonly found in junior and senior high schools, tracking often begins in elementary schools with the placement of students in high, middle, and low reading and math groups. In the secondary schools the groups are sometimes labeled college bound, academic, vocational, general, and remedial. Critics argue that track-ing robs students of equal opportunities and that negative stereo-types are often attached to the middle and lower groups.

See ABILITY GROUPING and DETRACKING.

Resources: *How to Untrack Your School,* P. George. Available from ASCD, 1250 N. Pitt St., Alexandria, VA 22314-1453, tel. 703/549-9110, or 800/933-2723. Internet: http://www.ascd.org

Tracking: Road to Success or Dead End? two audiotapes. Available from ASCD, 1250 N. Pitt St., Alexandria, VA 22314-1453, tel. 703/549-9110, or 800/933-2723. Internet: http://www.ascd.org

trade books Individual novels and storybooks that are available for purchase at most retail bookstores. More teachers are incorporating trade books into their lessons, especially in English and history, to create more varied and interesting units of study.

tuition tax credit See VOUCHER.

ungraded school   See NONGRADED SCHOOL.

untracking   See DETRACKING.

values education   See CHARACTER EDUCATION.

visualization   Consciously creating a picture of something in the mind. Teachers sometimes encourage students to visualize situations to help them remember information or to prepare them for creative activities such as writing stories. For example, a history teacher might ask students to imagine themselves at Gettysburg on the morning before a day of heavy fighting, asking them to think about the sights, the sounds, and the smells around them, and how they would be feeling. Then, still pretending to be Civil War soldiers, the students might write a letter to a parent or friend about the battle of Gettysburg.

vocational education   Alternative schooling at the high school level that allows students to spend a part of the school day attending traditional classes and the rest of the day learning a trade, such as auto repair or cosmetology. Vocational classes may be held in the same school building as the other classes, or in a separate vocational-technical school. Students may also train at real work sites.

Vocational education has been thought of as a track (see TRACKING) for lower-achieving students. With today's emphasis on the SCHOOL-TO-WORK movement, advocates are raising the importance and credibility of these programs, enabling graduates to move into skilled, better paying jobs. Variations, such as TECH PREP, prepare students to go on to at least two years of college or technical training after graduating from high school. See also SCANS REPORT.

voucher A certificate issued to parents that can be used as full or partial payment of tuition for any nonpublic school. Advocates of vouchers argue that citizens should not be required to pay both school taxes and private school tuition. Opponents say that using government funds for private religious schools violates the separation of church and state, and that vouchers will reduce public school funding.

whole language   A technique of teaching reading beginning with reading whole texts before examining words and individual letter sounds. Advocates believe it instills a love of reading more than does a strictly phonetic approach, which begins with drilling and memorizing the basic vowel and consonant sounds. Studies indicate that whole-language practices work well with children who are visual, holistic learners. See PHONICS.

Resources: Educating Everybody's Children: Diverse Teaching Strategies for Diverse Learners, edited by R.W. Cole. Available from ASCD, 1250 N. Pitt. St., Alexandria, VA 22314-1453, tel. 703/549-9110, or 800/933-2723. Internet: http://www.ascd.org

Making Meaning: Integrated Language Arts, videotape series. Available from ASCD, 1250 N. Pitt St., Alexandria, VA 22314-1453, tel. 703/549-9110, or 800/933-2723. Internet: http://www.ascd.org.

"Reading Styles: High Gains for the Bottom Third," by M. Carbo. *Educational Leadership,* February 1996, pp. 8–13.

world-class standards   This term is used in several contexts. Critics of U.S. education use the term by saying that U.S. students are "not up to speed with world-class standards," and they compare test scores of students in other industrialized countries with those of U.S. students as their proof. In this context it is seen as a movement to ensure that U.S. students measure up to the learning and achievement of students in other industrialized countries.

In 1993, the NEW STANDARDS PROJECT began to collect and analyze standard tests and documents from other countries whose students performed well on international tests and whose citizens perform well economically and tend to hold skilled jobs. The conclusion is that systems are successful when they set clear, consistent, demanding public standards that make sense in the culture of the school and the country. Performance assessments are also found in successful international programs, and teachers are more involved in exam creation and ASSESSMENT.

Resource: "Where in the World Are World-Class Standards?" by L. Resnick and K. Nolan. *Educational Leadership,* March 1995, pp. 6–10.

year-round schooling Replacing the traditional school year of nine months and a long summer break with a 12-month school year that includes several short breaks. Year-round schooling can accommodate changing lifestyles, beliefs about learning, and financial and overcrowding difficulties. The traditional school calendar reflects a society that needed children home in the summer to work on farms. In today's society, children are frequently left home alone in the summer with little to do.

Schools can adopt one of several year-round models. In the single-track approach, the lengthy summer vacation is replaced by several shorter breaks that are scattered throughout the calendar year. The advantage is that students retain more information than they would over a long break and need less review, so more learning is accomplished. The frequent breaks can also give both students and teachers more opportunities to relax without becoming bored. Some schools offer mini-courses and enrichment classes during breaks.

In a multitrack approach, school is always in session, but only a portion of the students attend at any one time so there is enough room to accommodate everyone. A school built to accommodate 750 students can be used to educate 1,000 students if, at any given time, 250 of them are on vacation. The multitrack method saves tax dollars by allowing for the extra students without building a larger school, but costs are accrued for salaries, maintenance, and air conditioning (as needed).

Another approach to year-round schooling extends the school year from its traditional 180 days to as many as 247 school days. Drawbacks of these methods, aside from considerable extra cost, are that family schedules and child-care arrangements are disrupted, at least initially. Breaks at nontraditional times of the year, however, may allow families to enjoy less expensive, less crowded vacations.

Resource: The National Association for Year-Round Education (NAYRE), P.O. Box 711386, San Diego, CA 92171-1386, tel. 619/276-5296.

Index by Topic

107

Curriculum

Diversity Issues

Family Involvement

Legislation

Organizations

Reform Terms/Methods

110

Research

School and Work

School Types

Staff Development/Supervision

Teaching Methods

The Authors

J. Lynn McBrien is Editor-in-Chief of *Education Today* and the Family Education Network Newsletter. She may be contacted by e-mail, irisht@tiac.net.

Ronald S. Brandt is Assistant Executive Director of ASCD and former Executive Editor of *Educational Leadership*.